MW01624950

The Art of Connectivity

Unveiling the Magic of NFTs

First Edition: August 2023

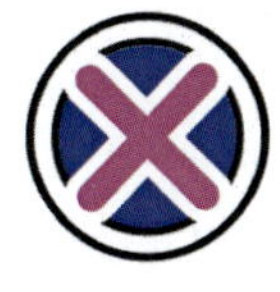

Amir Soleymani (Mondoir)

The Art of Connectivity: Unveiling the Magic of NFTs

The information and insights presented in this book are intended for educational and informational purposes only. The content herein is not intended to provide financial, investment, or legal advice. Readers are encouraged to conduct their research and seek professional advice before engaging in any financial or investment activities related to NFTs, cryptocurrencies, or blockchain technology. The views expressed by the author are based on their personal experiences and research as of the publication date, and the NFT space is subject to rapid and continuous change. The author and publisher are not liable for any decisions made based on the information in this book. Please be aware that the NFT market can be speculative and volatile, and readers should exercise caution and diligence when navigating this emerging landscape.

The images included in this book are sourced from NFTs owned by Amir Soleymani (aka Mondoir). It is essential to acknowledge that the intellectual property rights of these NFTs and artworks belong solely to their respective creators. The inclusion of these images is purely for illustrative and educational purposes and does not imply any ownership or transfer of rights. Any unauthorized use or reproduction of these artworks outside the context of this book is strictly prohibited. All rights are reserved by the original artists and creators of the NFTs, and any inquiries or requests for usage should be directed to them.

Self-Published
Cover design: Amir Soleymani

ISBN: 978-1-3999-6244-5

GM

In the world of Web3, GM is a delightful abbreviation for "Good Morning". It has become a cherished and signature way for individuals to begin conversations. This friendly greeting encapsulates the spirit of connectivity and camaraderie that permeates the Web3 community, where people from diverse backgrounds come together to explore the fascinating possibilities of blockchain technology and NFTs. So, with a warm "GM" in tow, Web3 enthusiasts embark on their daily adventures, united by their shared passion for this transformative digital frontier.

Dedication

To my loving wife, Hoda, your unwavering support and encouragement fueled my passion for the non-fungible token (NFT) space and made this book possible.

To my two wonderful kids, Adelia and Simon, for your unwavering love and inspiration. This book is dedicated to your future, where creativity, curiosity, and innovation will continue to shape the world.

To the vibrant NFT community, from artists to collectors, thought leaders, and enthusiasts, your creativity and dedication are shaping the future of art and technology.

To Farzin, Mehdi, Abdulla, Tom, Keith and Bala, you stood by my side throughout this journey, providing invaluable insights and friendship.

To Riyaaz, your guidance and assistance in writing this book were invaluable and are deeply appreciated.

To the memory of Jin Yu and Alotta Money, your pioneering spirit and vision in the NFT, Web3, and digital art space will forever inspire me.

And to all those who dare to dream, explore, and embrace the magic of NFTs, this book is for you.

In this book, there may be many artists, collectors, thought leaders, and friends whom I might have inadvertently omitted to mention. For any oversight, I sincerely apologize. Please know that I deeply value your friendship and contributions to the digital art ecosystem. Your presence has been instrumental in shaping my journey, and I hold the highest respect for each and every one of you.

Thank you for being part of this transformative adventure.

This technological revolution is not about changing what art is but about expanding the canvas of possibilities for artists and collectors alike.

Table of Contents

Summary 8
Introduction 11
The Intersection of Art and Blockchain 15
The Technology behind NFTs 22
Discovering NFTs 26
Building Connections 32
Using NFTs for Good 54
Facing Challenges 60
Collectibles vs. Art 74
Collecting Philosophy 82
Evolving as a Collector 89
The Myth of Decentralization 92
Influencers, Thought Leaders, and Regulations 98
The Future of NFTs and Digital Art 108
My Role in the Future of Digital Art and NFTs 120
Conclusion 123
Frequently Asked Questions 127
Bio 154
Proof of Reading Collectible 156

Summary

The Art of Connectivity: Unveiling the Magic of NFTs is a captivating exploration of the transformative power of Non-Fungible Tokens (NFTs) and their profound impact on the art world. With a passion for collecting and an insatiable curiosity about the intersection of art and technology, I embarked on a remarkable journey into the realm of NFTs, uncovering the magic and potential that lie within.

From the earliest memories of browsing my grandfather's stamp collection to embracing cryptocurrencies and digital assets, my path led me to the dynamic world of NFTs. Within this realm, I discovered a new dimension of art, where digital creations hold immense value and the possibilities for connection and collaboration are boundless.

The Art of Connectivity immerses readers in my personal experiences and encounters with renowned artists, influential figures, and a vibrant community of collectors and creators. The book showcases the transformative nature of these connections, highlighting the power of shared passions and collaborations that emerge in the NFT space.

As I delve deeper into my NFT journey, my collecting philosophy evolves. I will walk you through my transition from an initial focus on aesthetics to a more discerning approach, seeking artists who stay true to their unique style and artistic integrity rather than simply chasing trends. This book emphasizes the importance of valuing art and connection over financial returns and the rewarding experiences that come from supporting lesser-known artists.

Beyond the realm of collecting, I embraced the role of activism and personal growth within the NFT community. I have used my platform to raise awareness of important issues, participated in charity events, and made a positive impact. Through these endeavors, I discovered that in the NFT space, people and the community matter more than profits.

The Art of Connectivity delves into the controversies surrounding NFTs, challenging traditional notions of art and sparking discussions about the ever-evolving definition of creativity. The book invites readers to ponder the significance of digital art and its ability to evoke emotions, communicate ideas, and reflect the society in which it creates.

I will share my belief in the future of NFTs as a force for good and a catalyst for change. I will explore the possibilities of blockchain technology as a backbone for the art industry, providing trust, accessibility, and new avenues for artistic expression.

I am painting a compelling portrait of the NFT landscape, capturing the excitement, challenges, and memorable moments that define my journey.

The Art of Connectivity invites readers to explore the magic of NFTs, where connectivity, creativity, and the boundless potential of the digital age converge to shape the art world of tomorrow.

Introduction

In the ever-expanding digital landscape, a groundbreaking phenomenon has emerged, reshaping the art world as we know it. This book is the story of my odyssey into the realm of non-fungible tokens (NFTs) and the exhilarating journey that unfolded as I embraced the infinite possibilities of the digital art revolution.

From the dusty archives of my grandfather's stamp collection to the gleaming pixels of the digital realm, my lifelong passion for collecting found new life in the form of NFTs. As a child, I marveled at the tangible artifacts of the past, but it was the boundless potential of the digital age that captivated my imagination.

With the advent of cryptocurrencies, I delved into the world of Bitcoin and the decentralized technologies that underpin it. Little did I know that these early explorations would serve as the gateway to a realm where art and technology intersect in unprecedented ways. It was

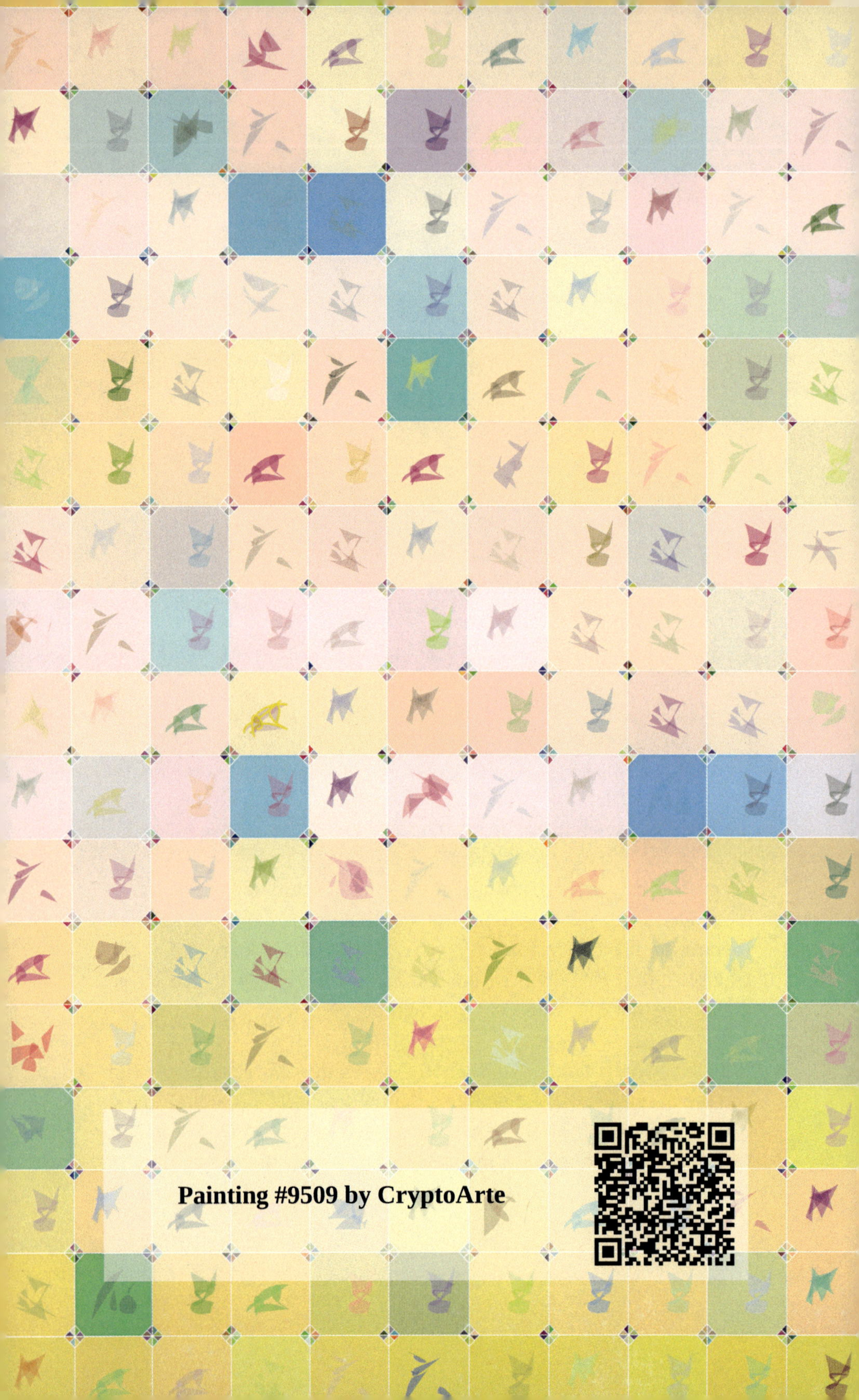
Painting #9509 by CryptoArte

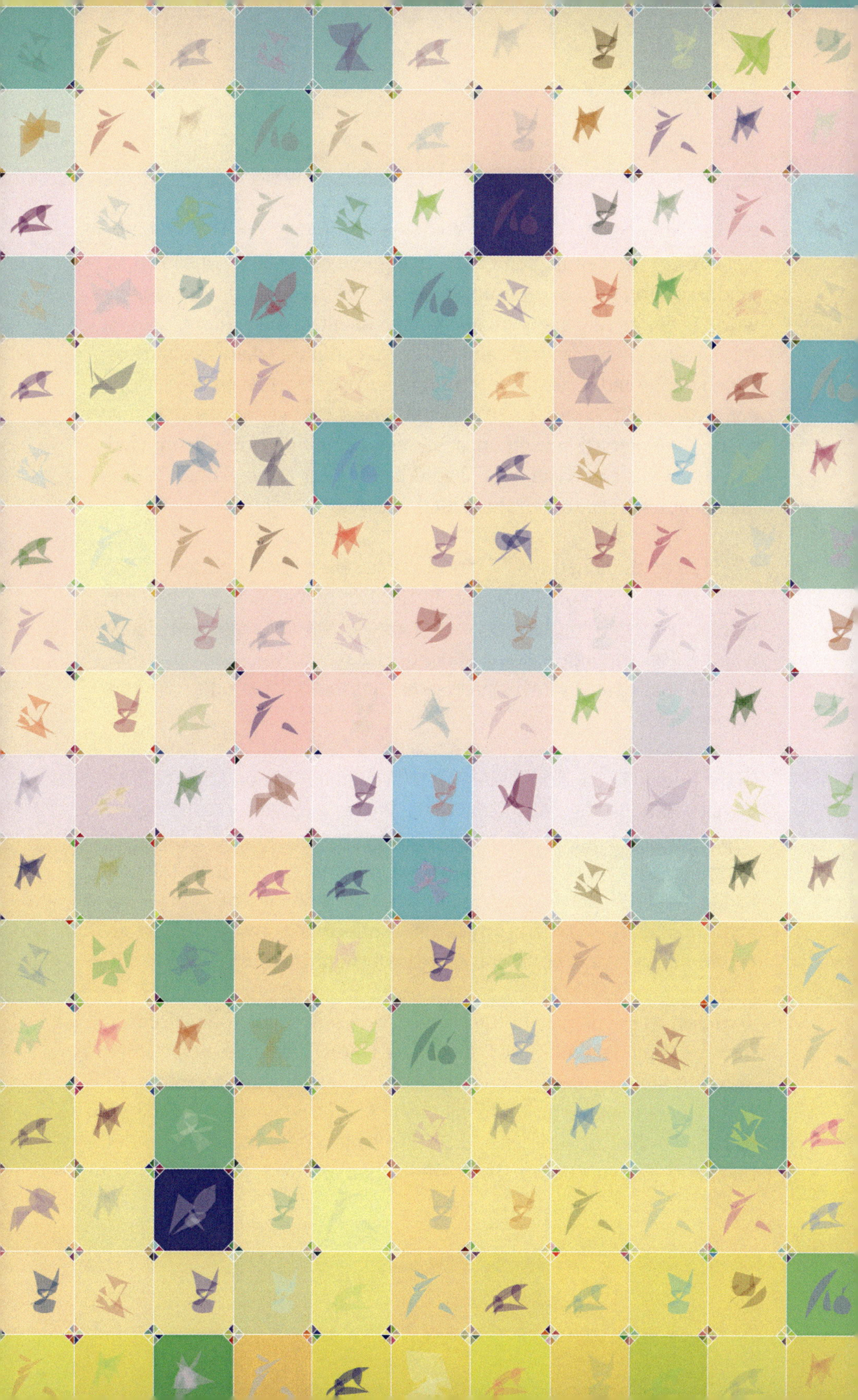

within this realm that I discovered the transformative power of NFTs.

At first glance, the concept of owning a digital asset may seem perplexing. How could something intangible hold such value? But as I embarked on my NFT journey, I quickly realized that this newfound world is not merely about ownership but about so much more.
It is a realm where art transcends physical confines, where the barriers of geography and accessibility crumble, and where artists and collectors converge in an explosion of creativity and connection. Within this space, I immersed myself in a vibrant community of like-minded individuals, each driven by a shared passion for art, technology, and the boundless potential of the digital frontier.

My journey through the NFT landscape has been challenging, though. The pressures of collecting, the intricacies of navigating a nascent market, and the constant evolution of technology have tested my resolve. But through these challenges, I have grown, evolving from a collector driven by investment potential to a champion of art and community.

In the following pages, I invite you to accompany me on a compelling voyage through the world of NFTs. We will explore the profound impact of this digital revolution on the art world, witnessing the birth of new art forms and the rise of a global community united by a shared vision. We will delve into the exhilarating moments of connection and collaboration, where artists and collectors converge to create extraordinary works of art and forge enduring friendships.

Together, let us uncover the transformative power of NFTs and discover the vast potential within this brave new world. This book is the story of how a simple passion for collecting led me down an extraordinary path, where the boundaries of art, technology, and community merge to reshape the art landscape for future generations. Welcome to the uncharted territories of NFTs and the digital art revolution.

The Intersection of Art and Blockchain

At its core, blockchain technology offers transparency and security that can revolutionize multiple sectors, and art is no exception. NFTs allow digital artworks to be tokenized, offering an immutable record of provenance and ownership. This is a game-changer in the art world.

In the traditional art world, provenance and authenticity have been long-standing issues that have posed challenges for artists, collectors, and buyers alike.

Traditional art market records can be fragmented, incomplete, or lost over time, making it difficult to trace the ownership history and lineage of an artwork. This lack of provenance can raise doubts about the authenticity and legal ownership of a piece.

The art world has experienced numerous instances of forgeries and counterfeits, where fake artworks are passed off as genuine originals.

Without reliable and transparent provenance records, buyers may unknowingly purchase fraudulent pieces.

Stolen artworks can enter the art market, creating ethical and legal issues for buyers and sellers. The absence of a comprehensive and transparent provenance system makes it challenging to identify stolen pieces and return them to their rightful owners.

Art authentication is a subjective process that varies among experts and institutions. Differences in opinions can lead to disputes over an artwork's authenticity, causing uncertainty for potential buyers.

The painting *Salvator Mundi,* attributed to Leonardo da Vinci, has become one of the most controversial and debated artworks in recent times. Its history is shrouded in mystery, adding to the intrigue surrounding its authenticity.

In 2017, the painting gained global attention when it was sold at auction by Christie's for $450 million, making it the most expensive artwork ever sold at that time. The buyer was later revealed to be Crown Prince Mohammed bin Salman of Saudi Arabia, who intended to display it in the newly opened Louvre Abu Dhabi.

However, even before the auction, art critics and experts had been split on whether *Salvator Mundi* was indeed an original work by Leonardo da Vinci. The painting had undergone extensive restoration and conservation efforts over the years, which raised questions about its original condition and authenticity.

This authenticity debate underscores the challenges the art world faces in verifying the provenance and authenticity of valuable artworks. However, it also serves as a compelling argument for the potential of blockchain technology in resolving such issues.

If the provenance and history of “Salvator Mundi” had been recorded on a blockchain at the time of its creation, every transaction, restoration, and owner change would have been permanently recorded and transparently accessible. This immutable record on the blockchain would have provided a tamper-proof, verifiable trail of the artwork’s journey through history, leaving no room for doubt about its authenticity.

The traditional art market often involves numerous intermediaries, such as galleries, dealers, and auction houses. Each transfer of ownership can create a complex chain of custody, making it challenging to verify the authenticity and provenance of an artwork.

NFTs address these problems by leveraging blockchain technology to provide a secure and transparent solution for recording an artwork’s provenance and authenticity.

Each artwork is assigned a unique NFT, representing a digital certificate of ownership stored on a blockchain. Every transaction involving the artwork, from its creation to each subsequent sale, is recorded on the blockchain in a transparent and immutable manner. This creates a complete and tamper-proof provenance history that can be easily verified.

NFTs leverage cryptographic algorithms to secure artwork data on a blockchain, ensuring unalterable records of origin, ownership, and certification and instilling trust in the authenticity of each piece.

By eliminating intermediaries, NFTs empower artists with direct engagement–allowing them to tokenize and sell their digital or physical works directly to global collectors through blockchain platforms, thereby expanding their reach and recognition.

With NFTs, artists can transcend physical gallery limitations, gaining

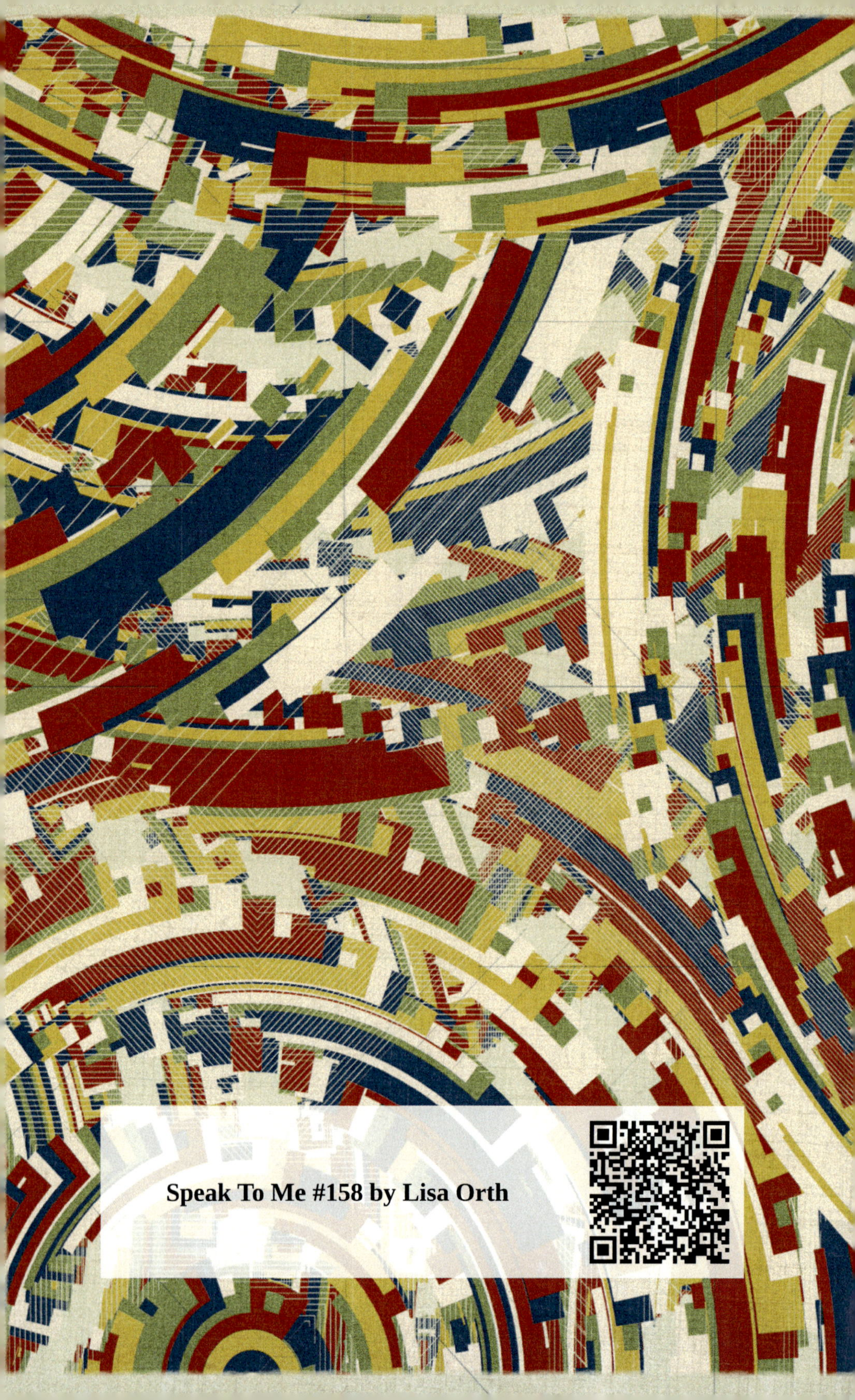
Speak To Me #158 by Lisa Orth

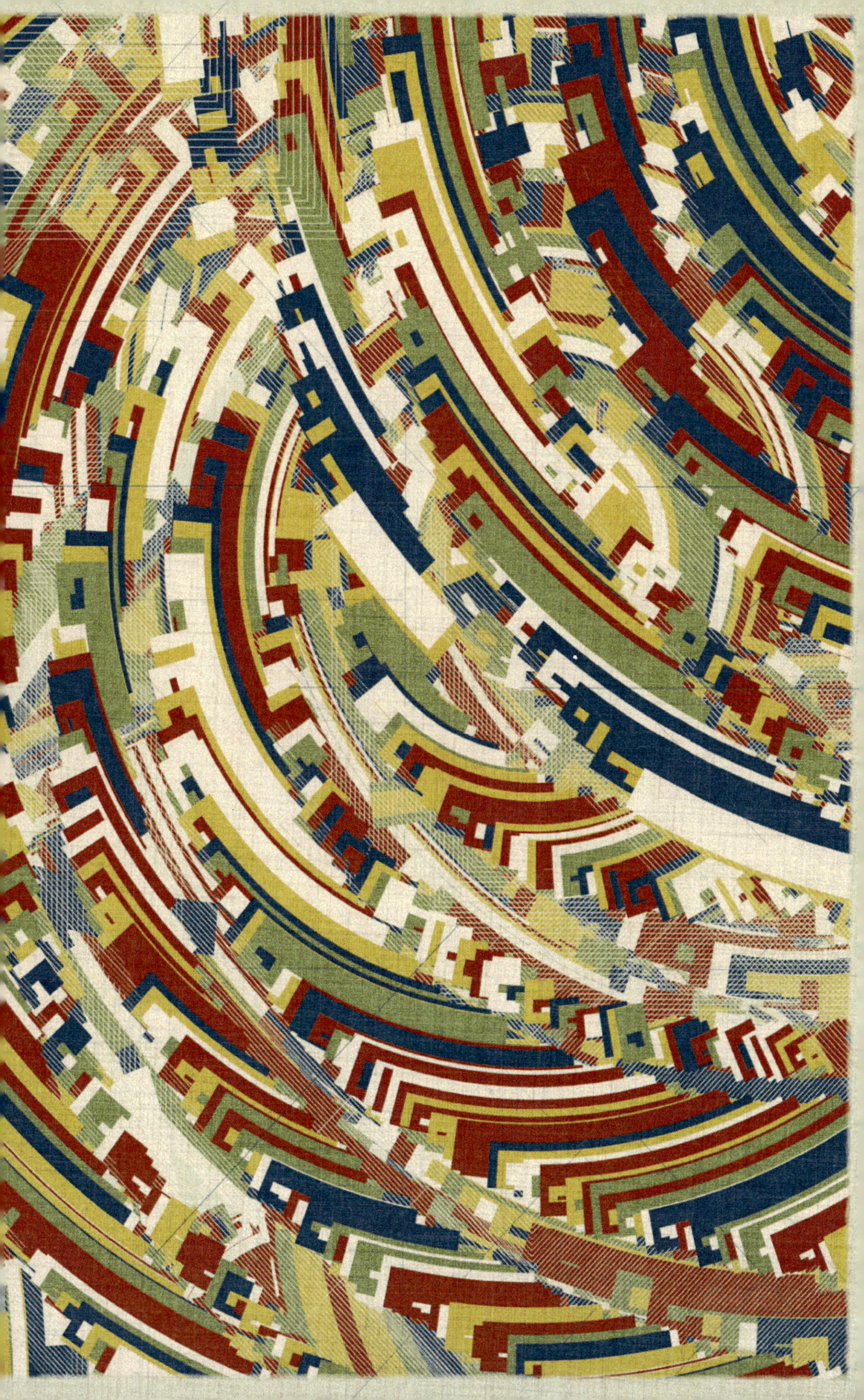

exposure to a worldwide audience, unlocking new opportunities, and increasing their visibility and impact.

The integration of smart contracts with NFTs enables artists to receive automatic royalties with each resale, ensuring ongoing benefits from the increasing value of their creations over time.

Art has long been a domain in which provenance and authenticity are paramount. Traditionally, these issues have been fraught with uncertainty, with rampant art forgery, and disputes over ownership. NFTs address these problems, allowing anyone to verify an artwork's history and ownership through a decentralized and immutable ledger.

But the potential of NFTs in the art world extends far beyond these technicalities. The real value of NFTs lies in how they have democratized the art world. They have opened the doors to countless artists who might otherwise have been left out of the traditional art establishment.

Through NFTs, artists no longer have to depend solely on galleries or middlemen to showcase their work. They can mint their own NFTs, sell their artworks directly to collectors, and have total control over their art. This shift is empowering artists like never before, giving them a platform to showcase their creativity and reach a global audience.

As an art collector, I have had the privilege of discovering numerous talented artists, many of whom might have been overlooked in the traditional art world. My art collection is not just a gallery of digital art; it is a mosaic of diverse voices and creative visions that represent the transformative power of this technology.

However, as much as NFTs have democratized art, they have also brought new challenges. As the NFT art space grows exponentially, so does the struggle for artists to be noticed among the crowd. This issue is close to my heart, and I am deeply passionate about finding solutions. It has become a cornerstone of my work in the NFT space, where I am dedicated to building tools and platforms that facilitate artist discovery, nurture creativity, and foster meaningful connections between artists and collectors.

NFTs have ushered in a new era of artistic expression due to blockchain technology, decentralization, and community engagement. The impact of this convergence extends beyond the art world, as it paves the way for new models of ownership, value creation, and collaboration in the digital age.

In my perspective, traditional art captures only a fleeting moment, freezing a glimpse of what the artist envisioned while crafting their masterpiece. To grasp the complete essence and comprehend how diverse elements intertwine and contribute to the whole, one must engage the artist directly and seek their insights. On the other hand, digital art provides artists with a myriad of creative avenues, such as animations, to add depth and dimension to their work, facilitating the effective communication of messages and fostering meaningful connections with viewers who can interpret the artwork in their own unique ways.

NFTs and the technology that underpins them can seem complex and intimidating, especially for those new to the world of cryptocurrencies and blockchain. However, once understood, the principles behind NFTs are pretty simple.

The Technology Behind NFTs

An NFT is a type of cryptocurrency that represents ownership of a unique digital asset. This can be anything from digital art to virtual real estate, music albums, or even tweets. What sets NFTs apart from other cryptocurrencies, like bitcoin or Ethereum, is that each NFT is unique and cannot be replaced with something else.

The uniqueness and indivisibility features are what make NFTs the perfect tool for digitizing art and other forms of creative work. By turning their works into NFTs, artists can create a digital certificate of ownership that is tamper-proof and easily verifiable. This solves a major problem in the art world, which has long struggled with issues of forgery and disputes over provenance.

The key technology behind NFTs is blockchain, a type of distributed ledger that records transactions across many computers so that any involved record cannot be altered retroactively without altering all

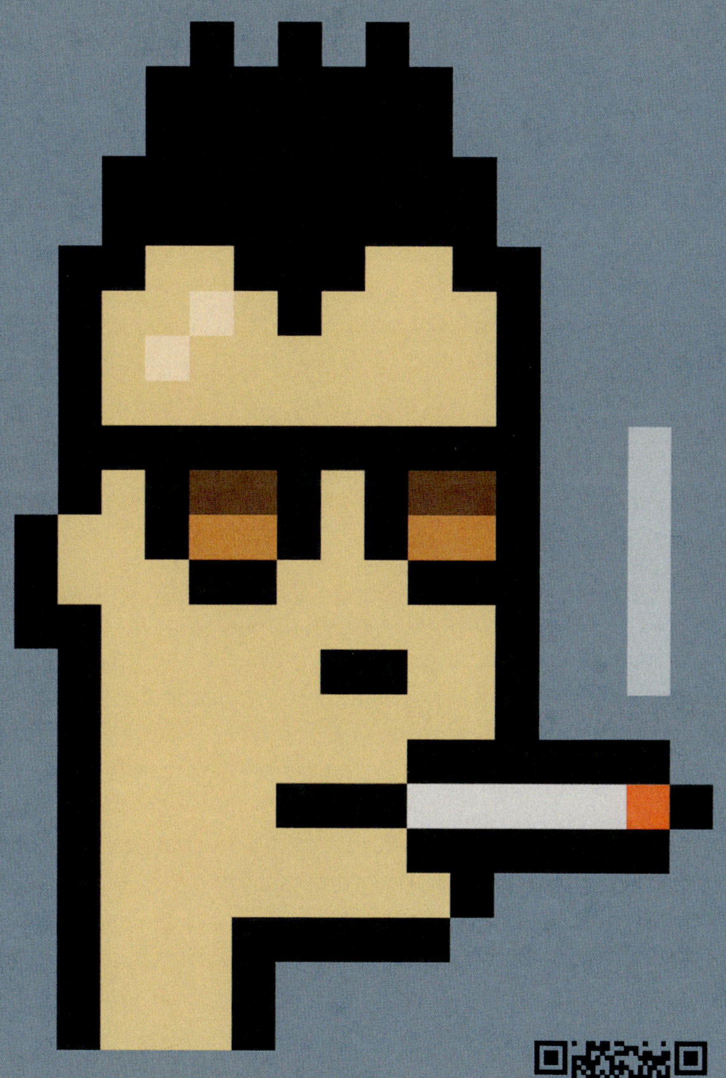

CryptoPunk #1704 by Larva Labs

subsequent blocks. This helps ensure the integrity and security of the data. Blockchain technology provides a transparent and decentralized infrastructure that allows for the secure storage and transfer of digital assets, eliminating the need for intermediaries and enabling direct peer-to-peer transactions.

Though blockchain technology originated in the world of finance, its applications are far-reaching. In the art world, it offers a revolutionary new way to create, buy, sell, and collect art. It allows artists to interact directly with their audiences, sidestepping traditional gatekeepers like galleries and auction houses. Artists can retain more control over their works and connect with collectors on a more personal level.

One of the key advantages of NFTs and blockchain-backed art is the democratization of the art market. Artists who were previously overlooked by traditional systems can now showcase their works and find a global audience. Collectors can discover and support emerging talents worldwide, fostering a more diverse and inclusive art ecosystem.

Generative art, a captivating form of digital art created through algorithms and computer code, has received a significant boost from NFT technology. Unlike traditional art forms like painting or sculpting, generative art emerges from the artist's skill in crafting or manipulating code, resulting in unique and ever-changing artworks. The process often incorporates elements of randomness or interactivity, paving the way for the creation of an infinite array of variations and rendering each piece of generative art truly one of a kind.

NFTs play a pivotal role in elevating generative art to new heights. By inscribing these mesmerizing pieces of code on a blockchain, NFTs bring a sense of permanence, uniqueness, and irrefutable provenance to each creation. Through the rise of NFTs, people around the world have begun to recognize and appreciate the inherent beauty and significance of generative art.

The marriage of generative art and NFTs has unlocked a world of possibilities for both artists and collectors. For artists, it offers a novel means of self-expression, combining artistic talent with technical prowess to create endlessly evolving masterpieces. On the other hand, collectors have the privilege of owning digital artworks that are not only visually mesmerizing but also intrinsically backed by blockchain technology, ensuring their authenticity and rarity.

Moreover, blockchain-backed art does not just have the potential to democratize the art market; it can also make the act of collecting more accessible, affordable, and environmentally friendly. The digital nature of NFTs reduces the need for physical transportation, storage, and insurance, lowering the associated costs and environmental impact. Additionally, the ability to store a verifiable record of ownership on a blockchain makes it easier for collectors to prove the authenticity and provenance of their pieces.

NFTs are challenging traditional notions of art, ownership, and value. This opens up new possibilities for creators, collectors, and enthusiasts alike. The transformative power of NFTs and blockchain technology is reshaping the art landscape, fostering direct connections between artists and collectors, and enabling a more inclusive and transparent art market.

Discovering NFTs

From my earliest memories, I was exposed to the enchanting world of collecting through my grandfather's stunning stamp collection. Even at the tender age of six or seven, I sneaked into his room to marvel at the beautiful pieces of art and history carefully laid out in albums. It was an experience that had a profound impact on me, igniting my passion for collecting.

Inspired by my grandfather's collection, I began my own collecting journey by steaming off used stamps from envelopes and gathering them with care. By the age of nine, I went to our local post office in Iran and keenly purchased blocks of stamps, eagerly seeking the guidance of the kind clerk on which stamps to add to my budding collection.

As I grew older, my fascination with collecting expanded to include currency notes and coins. The allure of these tangible pieces of history and culture captivated me, adding a new dimension to my collection.

Inheriting the collector's gene from my father, I followed in his footsteps by gathering vintage vases, dishes, and even cars. My first car, a 1942 Ford Mustang, holds a special place in my heart, serving as a reminder of my early journey into the world of collecting.

As my interests evolved, I found myself drawn to rare books, spending countless hours exploring underground bookshops in search of hidden literary treasures. My love for artwork blossomed as I acquired a limited edition print of Yoshitomo Nara and a coveted piece by the elusive street artist Banksy, obtained after patiently standing in a queue in London.

Being deeply engrossed in the world of technology and crypto, I eventually stumbled into the realm of blockchain art. My first encounter with digital art on a blockchain came through MyCryptons, an early platform that caught my attention. Soon after, I delved into the world of Gods Unchained, where I learned about the groundbreaking concept of NFTs.

One day, a conversation with my art dealer in Hong Kong opened my eyes to the immense potential of NFTs. He encouraged me to explore DontBuyMeme.com, a platform where I could acquire tokens, stake them to earn pineapple, and potentially even acquire a piece by the esteemed artist Beeple. Although the Beeple piece remained elusive, this marked the turning point in my NFT journey.

Through DontBuyMeme.com, I had the pleasure of discovering an array of remarkable artists, including FEWOCiOUS, Odious, and Frank Wilder. Each encounter deepened my appreciation for the world of NFTs and the incredible talent and creativity that thrived within this digital realm.

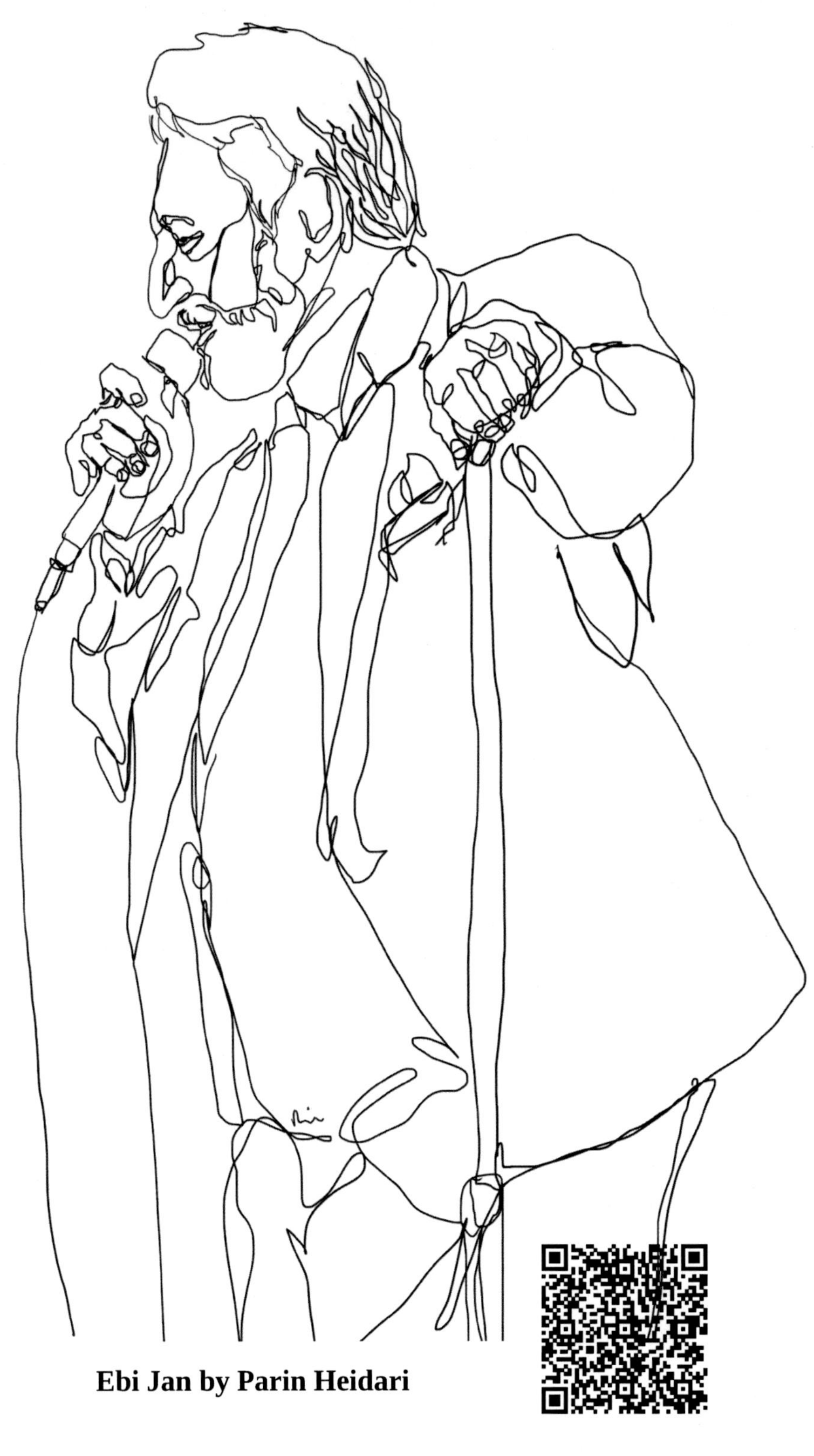

Ebi Jan by Parin Heidari

Thus, my journey into the world of NFTs had started, forever altering the trajectory of my collecting passion. From stamps and coins to tangible and digital artworks, each piece in my collection holds a story and significance that resonates with my heart and spirit. The world of NFTs has opened doors to boundless creativity, connections with talented artists, and the potential to redefine the future of art and technology.

When I first discovered the world of NFTs, I was drawn by the unexplored possibilities they presented. The idea of owning digital assets, particularly art pieces, was something I found fascinating. As someone who has always had a keen interest in art and technology, I was intrigued by the fusion of creativity and cryptography that the NFT realm represents.

Collecting digital assets was not new to me; I had already amassed countless items stored on my computer, phone, memory cards, and various storage devices. These comprised diverse code samples, internet images, gifs, memes, and many personal photos taken with my digital camera and phone. These were all digital assets that I had been accumulating. However, there was a significant distinction. My previous collections lacked a proper understanding of digital ownership. It was merely a process of downloading images from the internet without considering the concept of ownership meaningfully. However, with the advent of NFTs, the act of collecting took on a whole new dimension. It extended beyond mere downloads to encompass the experience of genuine ownership of a digital asset. The concept of proving ownership through blockchain technology revolutionized how I perceived and valued my digital acquisitions.

While the concept was undeniably novel, it was not just the technological appeal that captivated me; the concept of direct support for artists also resonated deeply. In the traditional art world, artists often struggle with visibility and financial stability. The NFT space, however, promised to change this paradigm by providing a direct, transparent connection between creators and patrons. I saw in NFTs an opportunity to support creators on a global scale and promote art forms that have been undervalued or overlooked in the conventional art world.

Vividly etched in my memory is the remarkable moment I experienced on Clubhouse, a social media app that facilitates live audio conversations and discussions. This exclusive platform required invitations for access, and I was fortunate to receive an invitation from my dear friend–Mo Malakoutian, with whom I used to play basketball in Iran during our 20s. On Clubhouse, I had the privilege of engaging in captivating conversations with friends, artists, and collectors, immersing myself in the vibrant art community.

This experience was entirely novel, and it revealed a whole new world of interactions for me. I had the privilege of speaking directly with the artist, delving into their inspiring narratives, understanding their creative processes, and being captivated by the beauty of their artistic mindsets. The urge to befriend these creators was irresistible, as their passion and dedication resonated deeply with me.

There were other instances on Clubhouse where I had the opportunity to listen to artists share their struggles. Many of them recounted their challenges, how the art world had rejected them for not conforming to norms or not adhering to the conventional paths of artistic exploration. Hearing their stories ignited a sense of empathy and compassion within me.

Being part of this digital community enabled me to play a positive role. I could intervene, offer support, and elevate these artists, becoming a source of blessing and excitement. Empowering these talented individuals on their artistic journeys and helping them break free from the constraints imposed by the traditional art world was an immensely fulfilling experience. Clubhouse became a platform for meaningful connections, advocacy, and celebration of creativity, leaving a lasting impact on my appreciation for art and the potential of digital spaces to nurture artistic talent.

The concept of spending digital currency on digital art felt like a bold leap into the future. The dynamic and fluid nature of the NFT market, combined with the promise of owning a unique piece of art immutably tied to me through a blockchain, felt like a compelling new form of patronage. The prospect of helping to shape a burgeoning artistic and economic landscape was exhilarating.

However, stepping into the NFT space was not merely a transactional decision for me. It was about more than investing in art or being part of a new technological wave. It was about being part of a burgeoning community of artists, collectors, and enthusiasts united by a shared interest in exploring this new frontier. The NFT world promised a new way to not just collect art but also connect with people worldwide.

Despite the unknowns and risks inherent in such a nascent market, my decision to dive into the world of NFTs was not driven by fear of the unknown but rather by a sense of curiosity and optimism. In NFTs, I did not see a risk but an opportunity– a chance to be part of a revolution, help shape the future of art, and join a community of pioneers exploring a new digital frontier.

Building Connections

The NFT space was like a bustling metropolis to me–teeming with creators and enthusiasts, each with a unique vision and story. It was not long before I realized that owning digital art was just the tip of the iceberg. The real treasure was the connections I was making, the relationships I was building, and the collaborations I was participating in.

Thanks to my involvement in the world of NFTs, I had the privilege of crossing paths with several remarkable individuals who have profoundly impacted my life. Allow me to share some of the most influential people I have encountered throughout this transformative journey.

Jin Yu, better known as WolfXLion in the NFT world, was an extraordinary individual and a dear friend. Sadly, he passed away due to COVID-19, leaving behind a rich legacy in the NFT community.

Jin was not only an inspiring friend but also a connector. He was instrumental in fostering my friendships with influential figures like Keith Grossman, Paris Hilton, and Nadya Tolokonnikova, a founding member of the feminist group Pussy Riot. His absence is profoundly felt, and his impact on the NFT space remains unparalleled.
My adventure in the NFT space began with an unexpected Twitter direct message from Farokh Sarmad, which marked the exciting start of this wild ride. Little did I know that this would be the beginning of a fascinating journey into the world of digital art and unique experiences.

Farokh and I developed a strong bond, united by our shared passion for the NFT space. Farokh, a prominent entrepreneur and a respected Clubhouse host with a substantial following, brought a dynamic perspective to my understanding of NFTs. Our engaging discussions about the future of NFTs and our shared belief in their vast potential significantly influenced my journey in this remarkable realm.

Through Farokh, I had the privilege of meeting Paolo Moreno and Nicole Behnam, both of whom became essential pillars of my presence in the NFT space. Together, we formed a tight-knit group, having daily FaceTime meetings to explore ways to propel this space forward and extend support to creators in the community.

Farokh's entrepreneurial spirit and innovative mindset led him to found Rug Radio, the first decentralized media agency in the NFT space. This groundbreaking initiative further showcased his dedication to pushing the boundaries of what was possible in the NFT world.

The connections and insights I have gained through Farokh, Paolo, and Nicole have been invaluable in shaping my NFT journey. Their unwavering passion and commitment to the space, along with their visionary ideas, have been a source of inspiration and empowerment. As a collective force, we continue to explore opportunities to drive positive change, support creators, and foster innovation within the

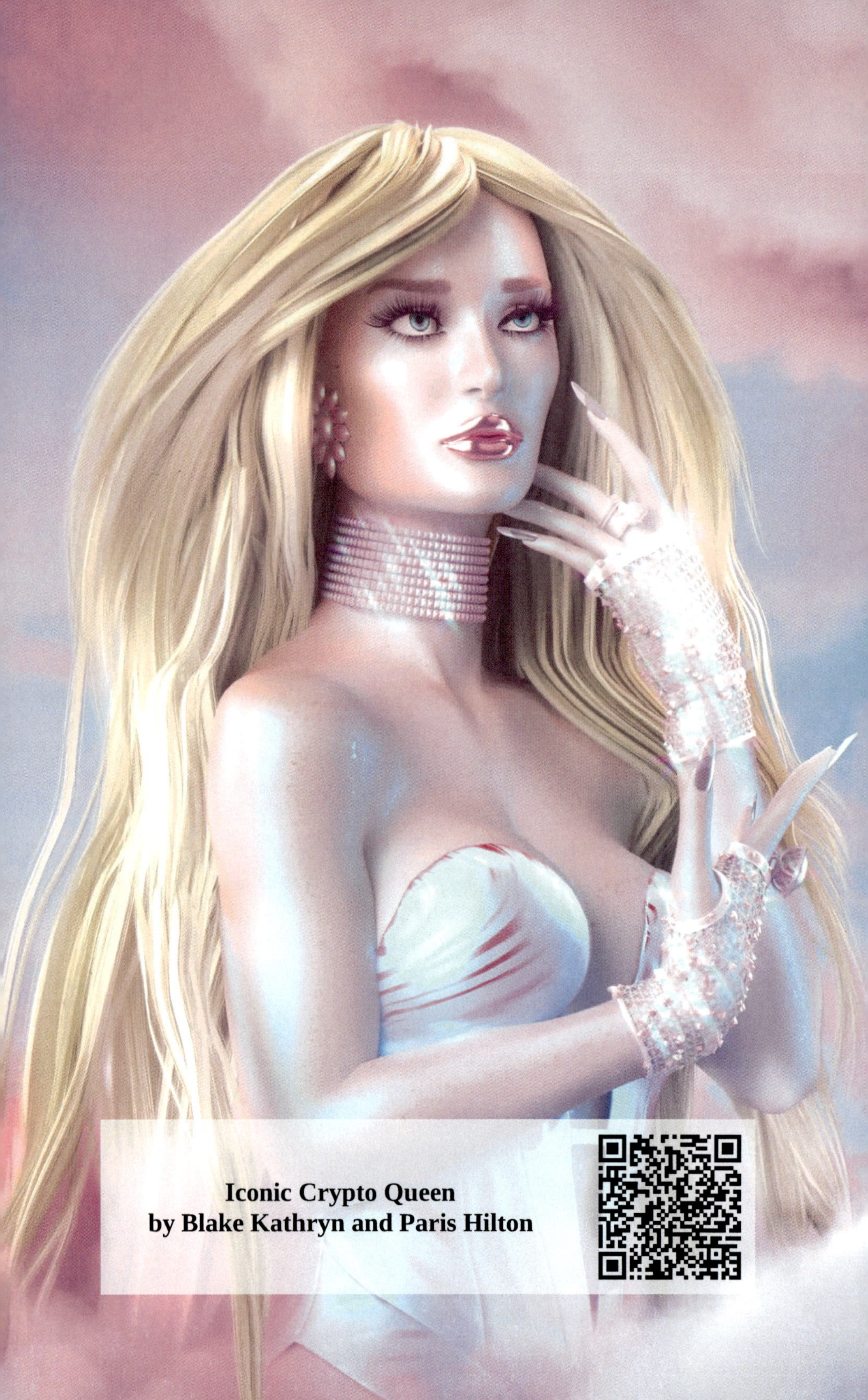

Iconic Crypto Queen
by Blake Kathryn and Paris Hilton

NFT ecosystem. The friendship and collaboration we share have been instrumental in navigating the ever-evolving landscape of NFTs and discovering the boundless potential it holds.

Paolo Moreno, a highly accomplished entrepreneur and esteemed thought leader, played a pivotal role in shaping my understanding of the NFT world. Our shared vision for the potential of NFTs and our profound discussions delving into the transformative power of these digital tokens deepened my appreciation for their significance. Paolo's insights and perspectives left a lasting impact on my approach and philosophy as an NFT collector.

Throughout our journey together, Paolo and I engaged in countless Zoom calls and FaceTime conversations. It was through Paolo that I had the pleasure of getting to know Carlos Luna James, also known as MGOGLKTKO. Carlos has become a treasured and close friend, and our conversations have spanned a wide range of topics, from art and spiritual elevation to politics.

One of the most memorable aspects of connecting with Paolo was the opportunity to engage with Sennett, also known as Mr. Checkpoint, on social media. Sennet is an inspiring activist in the US, passionately advocating for social justice. Through Paolo's network, I was fortunate to interact with this prominent figure, broadening my perspectives and understanding of important social issues.

Paolo's impact on my life extends far beyond friendship. He is also a highly experienced life coach, offering invaluable guidance and wisdom in both personal and business aspects. His mentorship has been a source of profound learning and growth for me.

Nicole Behnam, a well-known media host and a recognized figure in the NFT space, is another influential personality on my journey. Nicole's fresh perspective and passion for the NFT community always sparked insightful discussions. Her commitment to this novel medium and its potential for social impact further fueled my passion for the NFT space.

One of my most significant relationships is with Ryan, better known as ThankYouX. It is a connection that evolved from a mutual appreciation of art to a deeper understanding of each other's perspectives and visions. Our conversations often revolve around the NFT space's potential, its challenges, and how we could contribute to its growth and maturity. This relationship is not just about collecting his artwork but also about learning and growing together in this dynamic domain.

Then there is Paris Hilton, a name that needs no introduction. After winning the Paris Hilton/Blake Katheryn collaboration piece, I received a voice note from her on Instagram. To say that I was star-struck would be an understatement. It was a surreal experience, but what followed was even more special. Our conversations transcended her celebrity status, focusing on her passion for digital art and her journey in the NFT space. It was a beautiful amalgamation of two different worlds.

Through purchasing the Paris Hilton/Blake Katheryn collaboration NFT, I discovered a more profound significance beyond merely connecting with these two prominent figures. The collaboration held the profound purpose of acknowledging and uplifting female creators in a space that has been historically dominated by men.

As an activist, addressing such gender disparities is a personal mission for me, and this NFT purchase provided a unique opportunity to contribute to this cause. By supporting this collaboration, I actively contributed to the growing recognition of female artists in the digital art world. It was heartening to witness their names being listed among the top-selling digital artists, marking a momentous achievement in their careers and reinforcing their importance in the industry.

This meaningful accomplishment not only celebrated the talents of female creators but also sent a powerful message about the importance of inclusivity and gender equality within the NFT space. By playing my part as an activist and supporter, I felt a sense of fulfillment, knowing that I had contributed to breaking down barriers and fostering a more equitable environment for artists.

My friendship with Keith Grossman, the then president of TIME, is another unforgettable experience. It all started when I bought three TIME magazine covers as they dropped their Genesis pieces. The common thread of interest in NFTs and digital artistry opened doors for a meaningful friendship. Keith's insights into the intersection of media, technology, and art were enlightening and sparked several thought-provoking discussions.

Thanks to Keith, my life has been enriched with connections to numerous influential and exceptional individuals, from C-level executives and decision-makers to spiritual and thought leaders. One of the most cherished friendships I formed through Keith is with Poonacha Machaiah. Words cannot express how blessed I feel to have him as a friend. Additionally, Keith introduced me to the incredibly talented Parin Heidari, who has become one of my closest and dearest friends. Through Parin, I had the pleasure of meeting Jake Andrew, a now dear friend I deeply admire. Another remarkable person I met through Keith is John Knopf, an exceptional landscape photographer.

The impact that Keith has had on my career and personal growth is immeasurable, and I will forever be grateful for the opportunities and connections it has provided. Through these friendships and associations, my horizons have expanded, and my life has been enriched with meaningful experiences and professional growth. The value of these connections and the influence they have had on my journey cannot be overstated, and I will always hold a deep sense of gratitude toward Keith.

Among the various artists I have had the pleasure of meeting and forming a friendship with, DeeKay stands out as a particularly memorable and impactful connection. From the early days of collecting his works, I admired his talent and creativity, and it was evident that he was already a successful artist with a strong presence in big brands and a substantial following on social media. His art resonated deeply with the masses, and I was delighted to be a part of his growing collection.

As our connection grew, we began to engage in extensive conversations, and I vividly recall a remarkable two-hour call we had on WhatsApp. The depth and breadth of our discussions were unparalleled–covering a wide range of topics, from art to technology. Getting to know this young and immensely talented artist was an absolute privilege, and I cherished every second of our engaging conversation.

It was evident that DeeKay's passion for art and technology was infectious, and his insights offered a unique perspective that enriched my understanding of both fields. As our friendship flourished, I found myself continuously inspired by his dedication to his craft and the artistic impact he made on the world.

Connecting with DeeKay, collecting his artwork, and forming a genuine friendship is an unforgettable journey. I admired his talent from afar, and getting to know him personally has allowed me to appreciate not just his artistry but also the depth of his passion and creativity. Our conversations are a true privilege, and his influence on my appreciation for art and technology has left a lasting impression.

Another cherished friendship that has blossomed through my NFT journey is with Parin Heidari. Parin is not only an exceptionally talented artist but also a genuinely humble and wonderful human being. Her unique gift lies in her ability to vividly portray real-world interactions through her mesmerizing art, especially her captivating

Oh, To Be Missed.

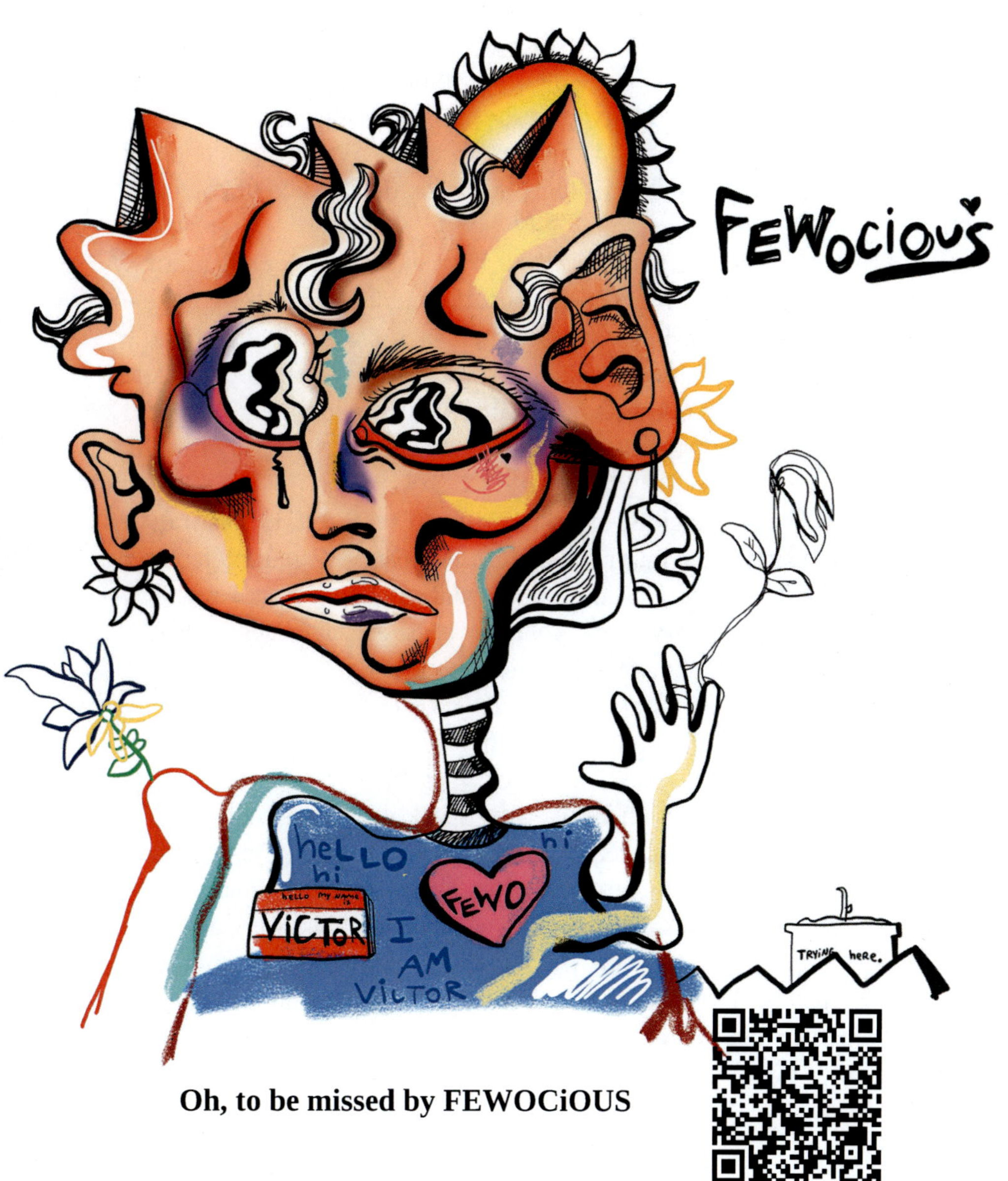

Oh, to be missed by FEWOCiOUS

visual representation of sound and music. The way she translates auditory experiences into beautiful and immersive artworks is truly awe-inspiring.

Similarly, I have had the honor of getting to know Jake-Andrew through NFTs. Jake, much like Parin, possesses a fascinating synesthetic perception where he sees colors through sound, music, and taste. This extraordinary gift is beautifully reflected in his abstract paintings, which present a stunning and distinctive representation of sound and taste through a vibrant and harmonious fusion of colors.

My friendships with Parin and Jake have enriched my NFT journey in profound ways. Their artistic talent, combined with their unique perspectives and insights, have expanded my appreciation for the boundless possibilities of NFT art. These connections are a testament to the genuine and lasting bonds that can be formed through a shared passion for art and creative expression in the dynamic world of NFTs.

Meeting Victor Langlois, also known as FEWOCiOUS, was truly a blessing in my NFT journey. One of the most profound interactions I had with him occurred during his remarkable auction at Christie's, where he made history as the youngest artist ever represented by the prestigious auction house. As I listened to his stories and participated in the bidding, fate smiled upon me, and I emerged as the winning bidder for the very last lot in the auction.

In a Clubhouse room where we were speaking, I could not help but ask,"So Victor, are you really coming to Liverpool?" This question arose because he had mentioned earlier that he would personally travel to the collectors of his pieces to deliver a suitcase filled with gifts. The room erupted with joy as the winner of the final lot was revealed to be me. Little did I know that this question would set a delightful sequence of events into motion.

Victor, along with ThankYouX, Cory Van Lew, and Odious, indeed made the journey to Liverpool to visit my gallery. I hosted a private party for Victor, showcasing the NFTs and the physical piece I had won in the auction. The moment he unveiled the suitcase brimming with hand-drawn paintings, heartfelt notes, and thoughtful gifts, a wave of joy, excitement, and accomplishment washed over me. It was a moment of shared laughter and tears as the genuine connection between us deepened.

To this day, Victor holds a special place in my heart. Our encounter was more than just an artist-collector interaction; it was a celebration of creativity, friendship, and the unifying power of the NFT community. The memories of that unforgettable gathering, filled with genuine emotion and camaraderie, remain etched in my heart as a testament to the beauty and magic of the NFT space.

Two of the most significant connections and friendships I established in the NFT space were with Joe Kennedy, the founder of the prestigious art gallery Unit London, and Kamiar Maleki, an influential art collector and advocate. Their expertise and passion for the art world enriched my understanding of NFTs and opened doors to new opportunities and experiences.

In addition, I have had the pleasure of forming friendships with Christian Burns, a talented musician from my hometown of Liverpool, and Brian Wayne Transeau (better known as BT), a massively successful musician and respected figure in the music industry. These connections with fellow musicians are especially meaningful, as we shared a mutual appreciation for both art and the NFT space.

Another unforgettable encounter was with Don Diablo, the renowned Dutch DJ and musician. During an auction for his Genesis NFT drop, I made a difficult sacrifice. Realizing that it would hold more significance for him if his first NFT was acquired by a fellow musician collector, I made the heartfelt choice to step back and call my oldest and dearest musician friend, Farzin. I shared the details of the piece with him and withdrew from the auction so that he could have the opportunity to win the artwork. This stunning piece is now in Farzin's prestigious music studio in Dubai.

Hamed Nikpay and Nik Yousefi are two of the dearest friends I have made through the NFT space. Both hailing from our motherland of Iran, Hamed is a widely respected musician, while Nik is a highly esteemed filmmaker. The bond we have formed through our shared passion for art and NFTs have been truly cherished and unforgettable experiences.

Discovering these talented individuals within the NFT community was a delightful surprise. Being able to connect with and support them in their respective journeys within the NFT space has been incredibly rewarding. Witnessing their artistic endeavors and creative contributions flourish in the digital realm has been a source of immense joy and pride for me.

Another significant connection I made within the NFT space was with Hamid Ebrahimnia, a highly accomplished and renowned Iranian Visual Effects Artist and 3D designer. Even before our encounter, Hamid's exceptional works and creations had garnered widespread recognition and appreciation from audiences worldwide. His talent led to noteworthy collaborations with superstars, adding to his reputation as a creative force to be reckoned with.

My initial connection with Hamid blossomed when I acquired one of his digital creations as an NFT. This acquisition opened the door to numerous engaging conversations between us. Recognizing the potential for creative synergy, we decided to embark on two collaborative NFT art drops.

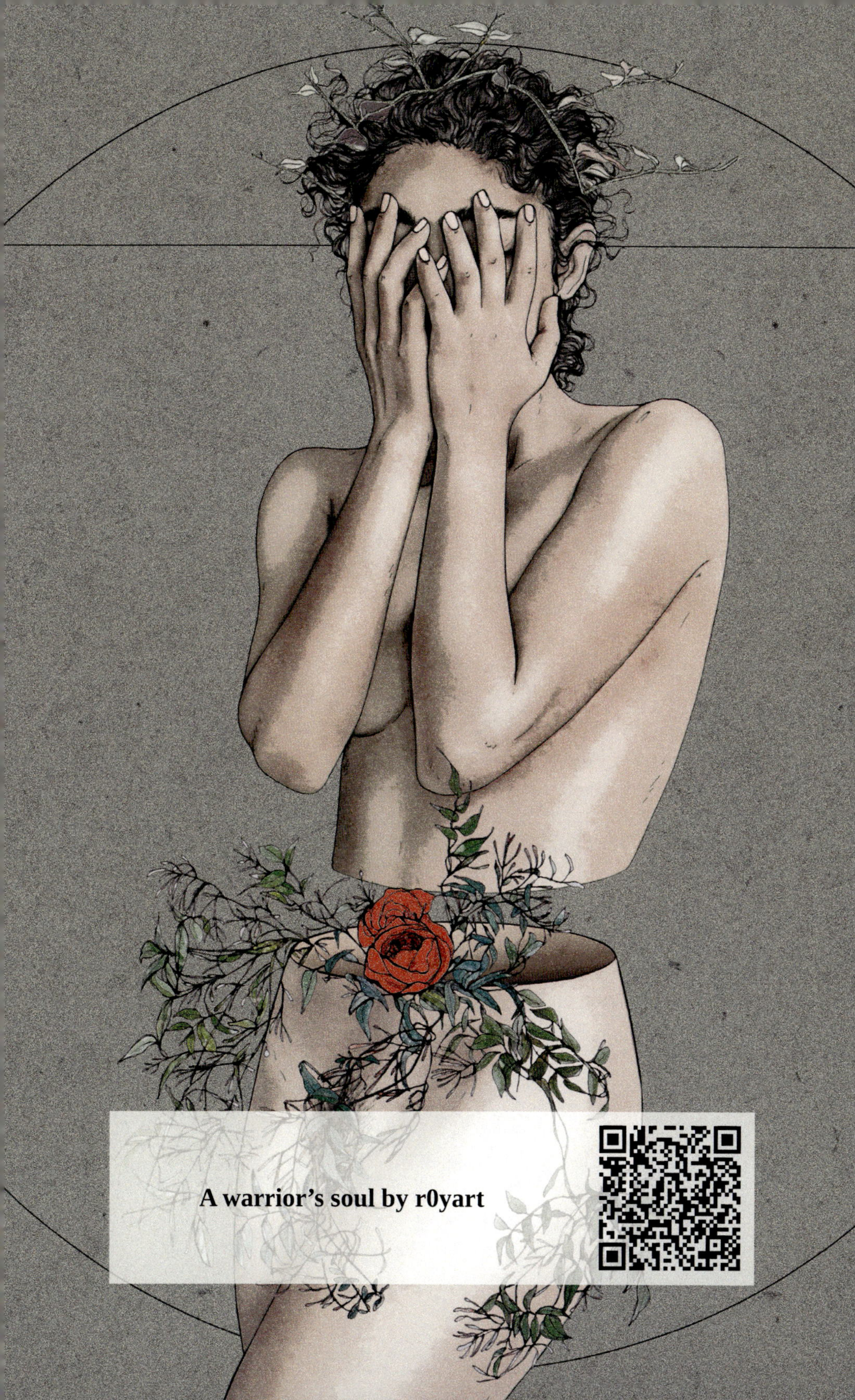
A warrior's soul by r0yart

The first collaboration gave birth to a stunning piece titled Crypto Art City, which holds a special place in my heart. The artwork beautifully merges our artistic visions and showcases the limitless possibilities of the NFT medium.

Our second collaboration was equally exceptional–as we joined forces to create a piece dedicated to Ebi, the famous superstar Persian singer. This project was a celebration of both art and music, and it exemplified the power of NFTs to bring artists and musicians together to collaborate and share their talents on a global stage.

Through these collaborations, I not only had the privilege of working alongside a creative genius but also formed a meaningful friendship with Hamid. Our shared passion for art and technology became the foundation of a strong bond that transcended geographical distances.

Mehdi Abbasian, a young and passionate fellow Iranian, stands out as one of the most profound connections I have made through the NFT space. With his successful entrepreneurial ventures and wizard-like abilities, Mehdi's presence has been a guiding light in my journey. Over the course of a year, we engaged in numerous conversations that strengthened our bond, and eventually, we joined forces to shape the future of Mondoir, my brand.

Through Mehdi, I had the pleasure of getting to know Abdullah Al Dhaheri, a dear friend and a valued member of the Mondoir family. Abdullah is a highly successful entrepreneur from the UAE, and our friendship has been an enriching and rewarding experience.

Moreover, Mehdi has introduced me to many incredible individuals, many of whom have become dear friends. Among them is the super-talented and legendary artist Sacha Jafri, whose artistic creations and talent I deeply admire. Additionally, I have formed close bonds with Tohi, an immensely successful Persian rapper, and his manager–Ali

Miri, whom I deeply admire. Moreover, thanks to Mehdi's introduction, I had the privilege of getting to know the super-talented artist Diaa Allam, a UAE-based calligraphy artist. Our shared interest in creative expression and art has brought us together, fostering a connection that extends beyond geographical borders.

It is astounding to realize how many friends I have gained solely through the NFT community. The NFT space has been a catalyst for these connections, allowing me to forge meaningful relationships with inspiring individuals from diverse backgrounds and creative domains.

Another fantastic friend I have had the privilege of knowing is Giuseppe Moscatello, an experienced art advisor and mentor with an impressive background in museums and institutions. His guidance and friendship were instrumental in the opening of my new gallery in Dubai. Without his invaluable assistance, this milestone would not have been possible.

Each of these friendships and connections has brought a sense of unity and camaraderie to the NFT community. Each of these moments has contributed to the tapestry of my NFT journey, weaving together a narrative of unexpected encounters, meaningful connections, and invaluable experiences. Through shared interests, passions, and creative endeavors, we have fostered genuine bonds that go beyond the realm of art and music. The NFT space has not only enabled me to collect valuable and unique pieces of art but also facilitated the creation of enduring friendships with like-minded individuals who have enriched my life in profound ways.

The NFT community–or as I fondly refer to them, my tribe–has become an integral part of my life. These incredible individuals are not just acquaintances; they are a part of me, ingrained in my journey and experiences within the NFT world. It is a profound bond of loyalty and love that I hold for these people who have become more than just

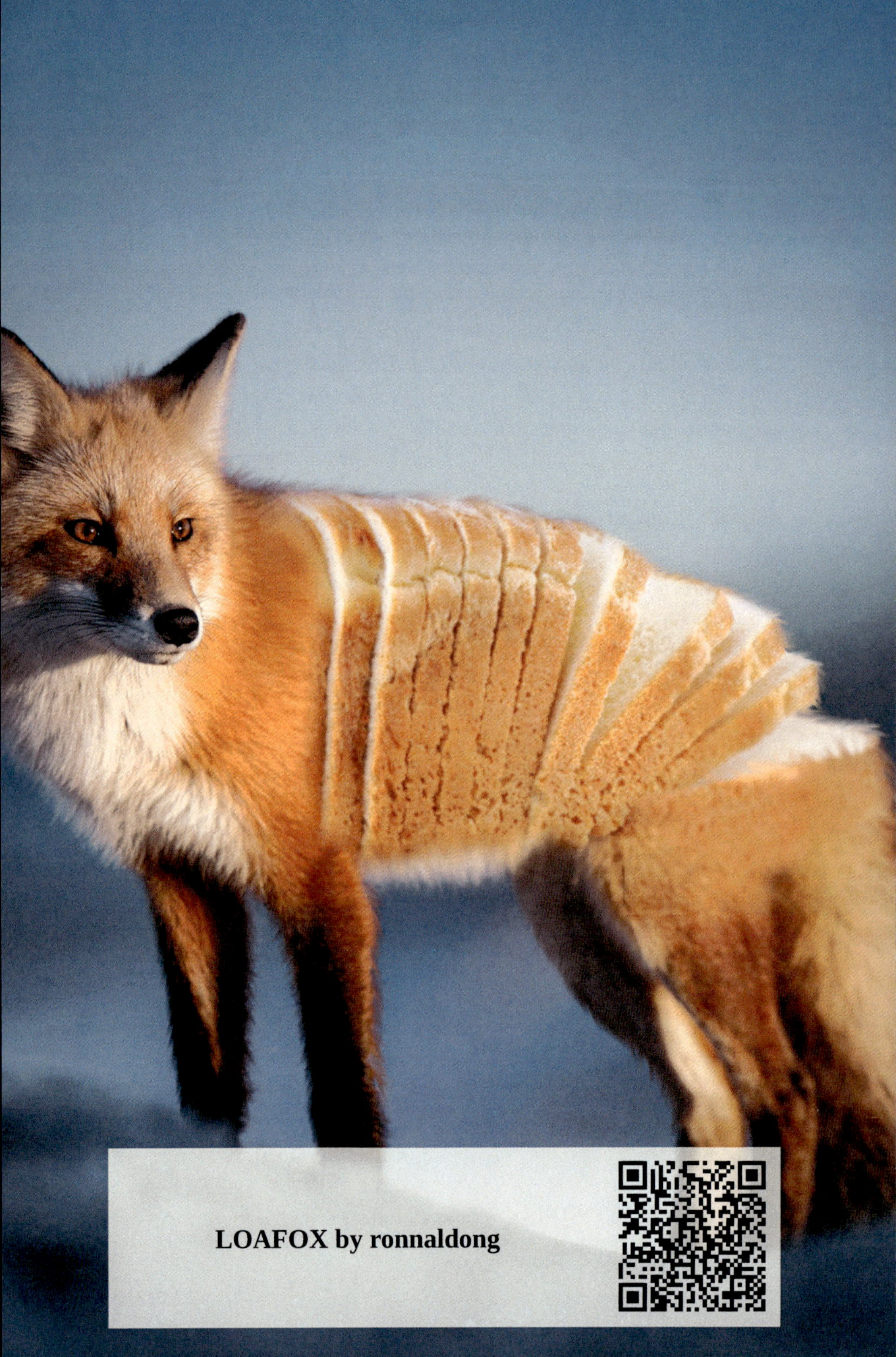
LOAFOX by ronnaldong

friends; they are family.

Their support, encouragement, and camaraderie have played a significant role in shaping my outlook on life and art. We share a common passion for creativity, innovation, and the transformative potential of NFTs. We uplift and inspire one another, celebrating our successes and supporting each other during challenges.

As the NFT space continues to grow and evolve, so does the richness of the friendships I have formed within it. These connections are a testament to the genuine and lasting bonds that can emerge from a shared passion and purpose. The NFT community has become a source of inspiration, motivation, and joy, and I am immensely grateful for the diverse and incredible individuals who have become an essential part of my life's tapestry.

These experiences reaffirmed that the NFT space is not just a marketplace; it is a thriving, nurturing community. The connections I was making were not transactional but meaningful and deep-rooted. Each relationship enriched my journey, providing new perspectives, wisdom, and a shared enthusiasm for digital art. I was not just a collector; I was part of a vibrant network of creatives and enthusiasts united by our passion for NFTs. It was this sense of community and connection that truly defined my journey in the NFT space.

Each of these connections enriched my journey in the NFT space in unique ways. The diversity of perspectives, the shared enthusiasm for the future of art, and the sense of community they helped foster are what truly make the NFT world an exciting space to navigate.

One of the most standout events in my career was the remarkable NFTLiverpool exhibition, an unprecedented five-month-long showcase featuring over 1,600 pieces of digital art at my gallery in Liverpool, UK. Initially, my art gallery was intended to serve as a private museum where I could enjoy and display my collection of physical art. However, as I delved deeper into the NFT space and recognized its potential for elevating artists, I realized the gallery could be utilized to support and showcase the incredible talents within the NFT community.

I took to Twitter and announced an open call, inviting artists from all walks of life to submit their digital creations for consideration. Simultaneously, I approached the influential friends I had made in the NFT space, requesting their participation as curators for the exhibition. Esteemed individuals from the worlds of business, art, and technology, such as Paris Hilton, Keith Grossman, ThankYouX, Joe Kennedy, PAK, Farokh and Kamiar Maleki, generously agreed to be part of this groundbreaking endeavor.

The response was overwhelming, with over 6,000 submissions from 4,000 talented artists. Collaborating with the esteemed curators, we embarked on the arduous task of selecting the most outstanding pieces, shining a well-deserved spotlight on 1,600 breathtaking creations. Throughout this process, we fostered new friendships and cultivated a culture of collaboration within the NFT community.

The NFTLiverpool exhibition was entirely self-funded. Although it was an immense burden, the experience proved to be worth every penny. Witnessing the art world come together in such a powerful and unprecedented manner was a testament to the transformative impact of NFTs and the boundless potential of collaboration and collective support.

By providing a platform for these talented artists to showcase their work, we not only celebrated their creativity but also laid the foundation for future opportunities and recognition within the NFT space. The NFTLiverpool exhibition remains a pivotal milestone in my journey, a testament to the extraordinary capabilities of NFT technology in reshaping the art world and fostering an inclusive and vibrant community of creators and enthusiasts alike.

One particular instance that stands out is when I had the privilege of speaking with MC Hammer in a Clubhouse room. Growing up with his iconic hit "U Can't Touch This," it was a surreal moment to have a conversation with a living legend, connecting on a platform that transcended traditional boundaries.

Another extraordinary moment that left me in awe was the day I received a direct message from Avant Arte on Twitter inviting me to a Zoom call to discuss Web3. As a long-time client of Avant Arte and a collector of their remarkable artworks, this was undeniably a milestone for me. The opportunity to engage with Avant Arte, a prominent player in the art world, on the subject of Web3 and the future of art and technology was both exhilarating and humbling.

Thanks to the support and connection of my dear friend, Abdullah Al Dhaheri, I had the incredible opportunity to sit with government authorities in the UAE and engage in discussions about Web3 and digital art. This momentous occasion marked a significant milestone in my journey, as it showcased how the NFT space is gaining recognition and attention from even the highest levels of governance.

Another extraordinary moment was having a telephone conversation with Jeremy Skule, the executive vice president and chief strategy officer of NASDAQ, to discuss Web3 and NFTs. This remarkable encounter came about through the introduction made by Keith Grossman, a valued connection in the NFT community. To have a conversation with such a prominent figure in the financial world about the transformative potential of NFTs was nothing short of extraordinary.

In October 2021, I received an invitation from Sotheby's to curate

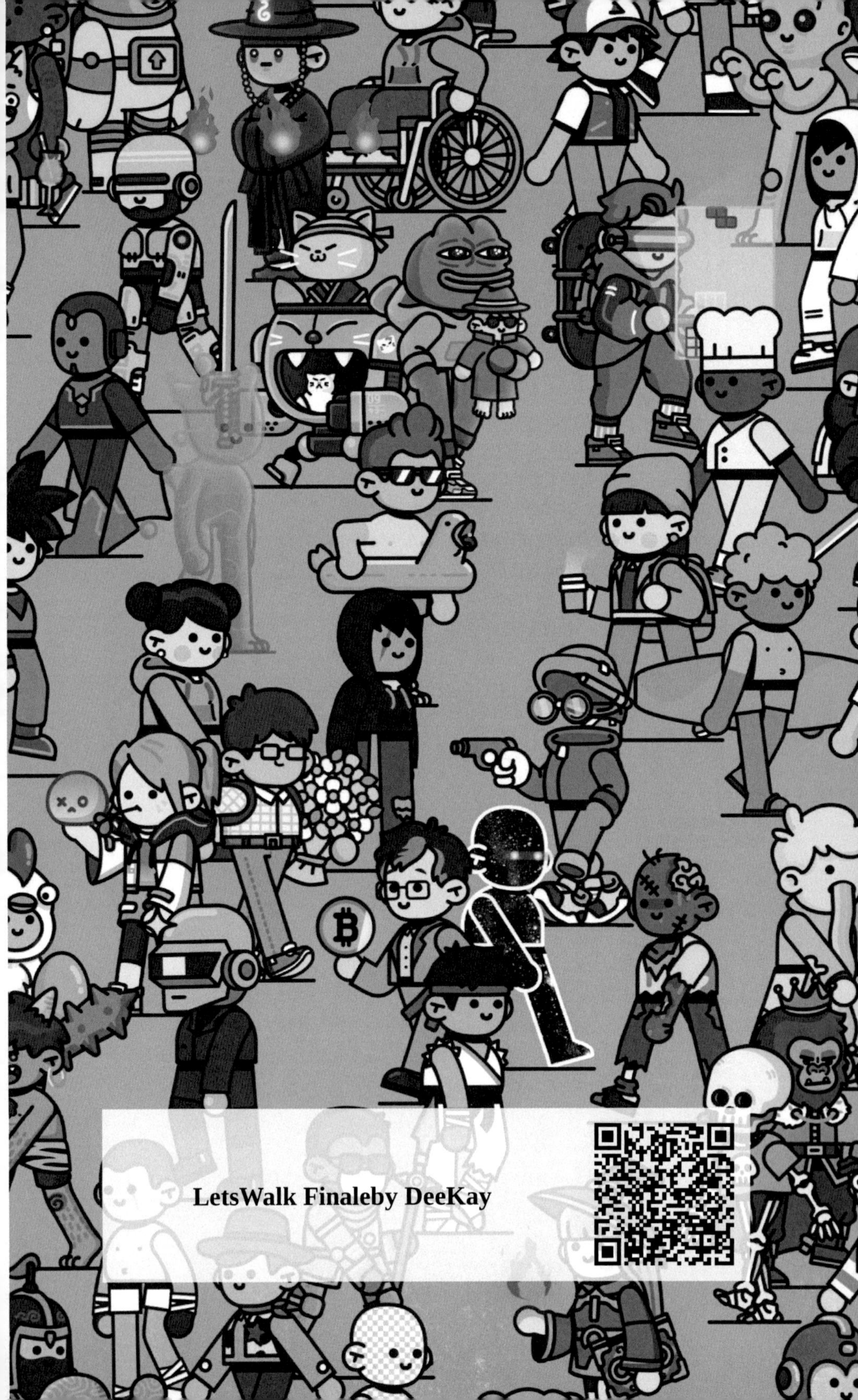
LetsWalk Finaleby DeeKay

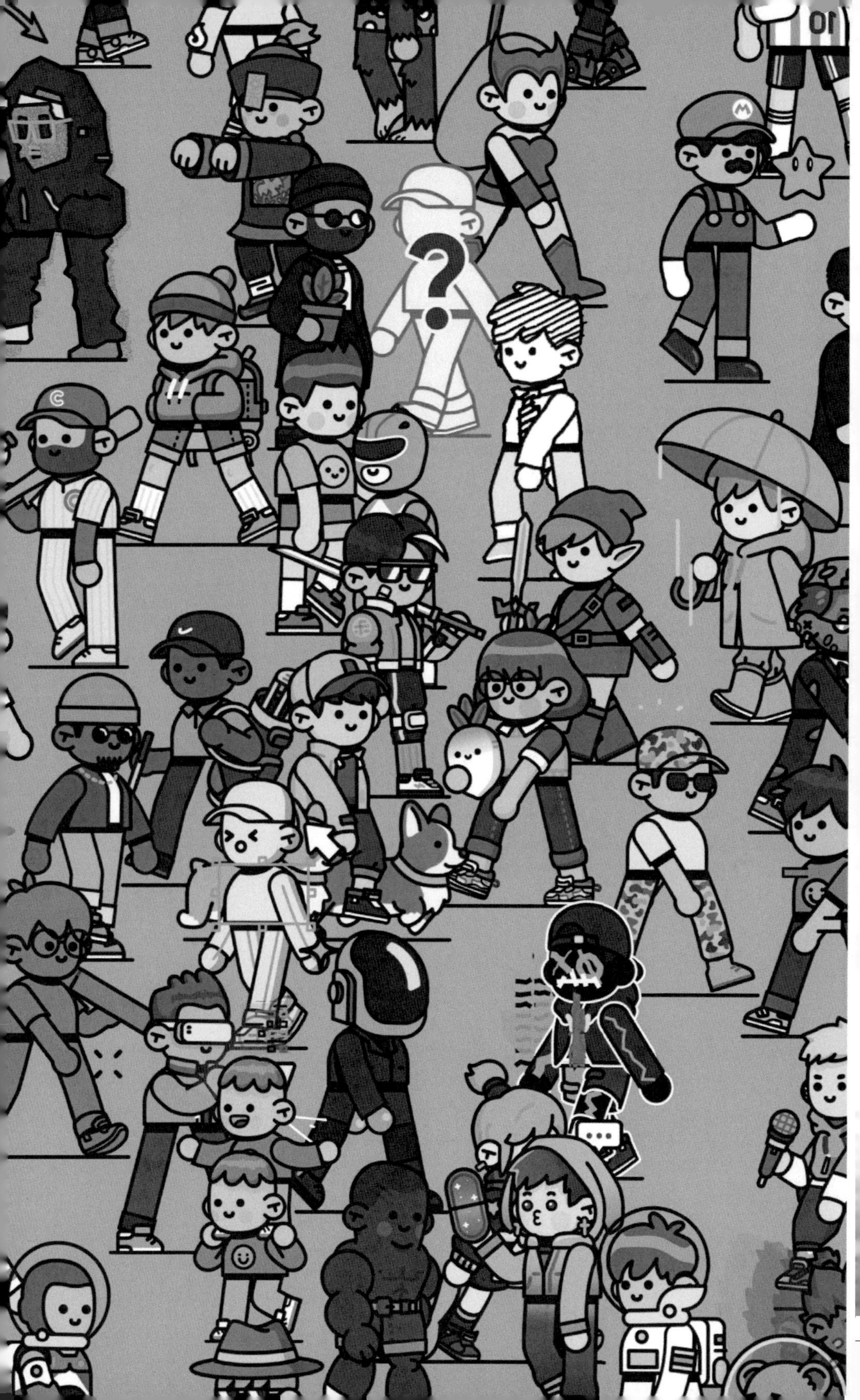

a selection from my existing collection for their Metaverse auction "Natively Digital 1.2: The Collectors". While they asked me to choose two existing pieces from my collection, I decided to bring two new works to the auction, aiming to benefit new creators rather than focusing solely on my own gains. As a result, I introduced Raphaël Erba and TIME to the auction, and it was a significant achievement for me, especially considering that it marked TIME's first participation in an art auction as an artist.

Additionally, I had the honor of being invited by Christie's to join their panel at their inaugural Art and Tech Summit in the UAE–part of Art Dubai 2023, where I had the opportunity to engage with industry leaders. It was a humbling experience to be recognized and to contribute to these prestigious events.

Furthermore, I was privileged to be selected for nftnow's top 100 list in both 2022 and 2023. The NFT100 is a recognition of the most influential creators and community leaders in the NFT space, and being part of this list is truly an honor for me.

These instances exemplify the impact of the NFT space and its growing influence on various industries, including finance, and governance. Being able to engage in meaningful discussions with government authorities and executives from renowned organizations like NASDAQ underscores the growing recognition of Web3 and digital art as significant forces shaping the future of technology, finance, and creative expression.

The NFT space has become a meeting ground for visionaries, artists, entrepreneurs, and industry giants. Through this digital realm, I have been able to interact with individuals who have shaped the business landscape and cultural zeitgeist, transcending boundaries and facilitating meaningful conversations about the transformative potential of NFTs.

These are testaments to the far-reaching impact of the NFT space and the dynamic potential it holds for fostering connections and propelling the worlds of business and art into new and uncharted territories. The journey has been awe-inspiring, and I eagerly anticipate the myriad of possibilities that lie ahead.

The NFT space has not only allowed me to collect digital art but also opened doors to unforgettable experiences and connections. The ability to engage with renowned personalities and legends across various fields has added a profound layer of richness to my journey, reminding me of the incredible potential of NFTs to bring people together in unexpected and remarkable ways.

Using NFTs for Good

I have realized that these digital assets have the potential to become a powerful tool for positive change. This understanding has led me to utilize NFTs to give back to the community, support those in need, and highlight the work of lesser-recognized artists.

Using NFTs for philanthropy, in my view, offers several compelling reasons that make it a powerful and impactful approach to supporting charitable causes.

Blockchain technology underlying NFTs provides a transparent and immutable record of transactions. Donors and participants in philanthropic NFT initiatives can easily track the flow of funds, ensuring that their contributions reach the intended beneficiaries.

NFTs revolutionize philanthropy by facilitating direct support for charities and social initiatives. When individuals purchase NFTs

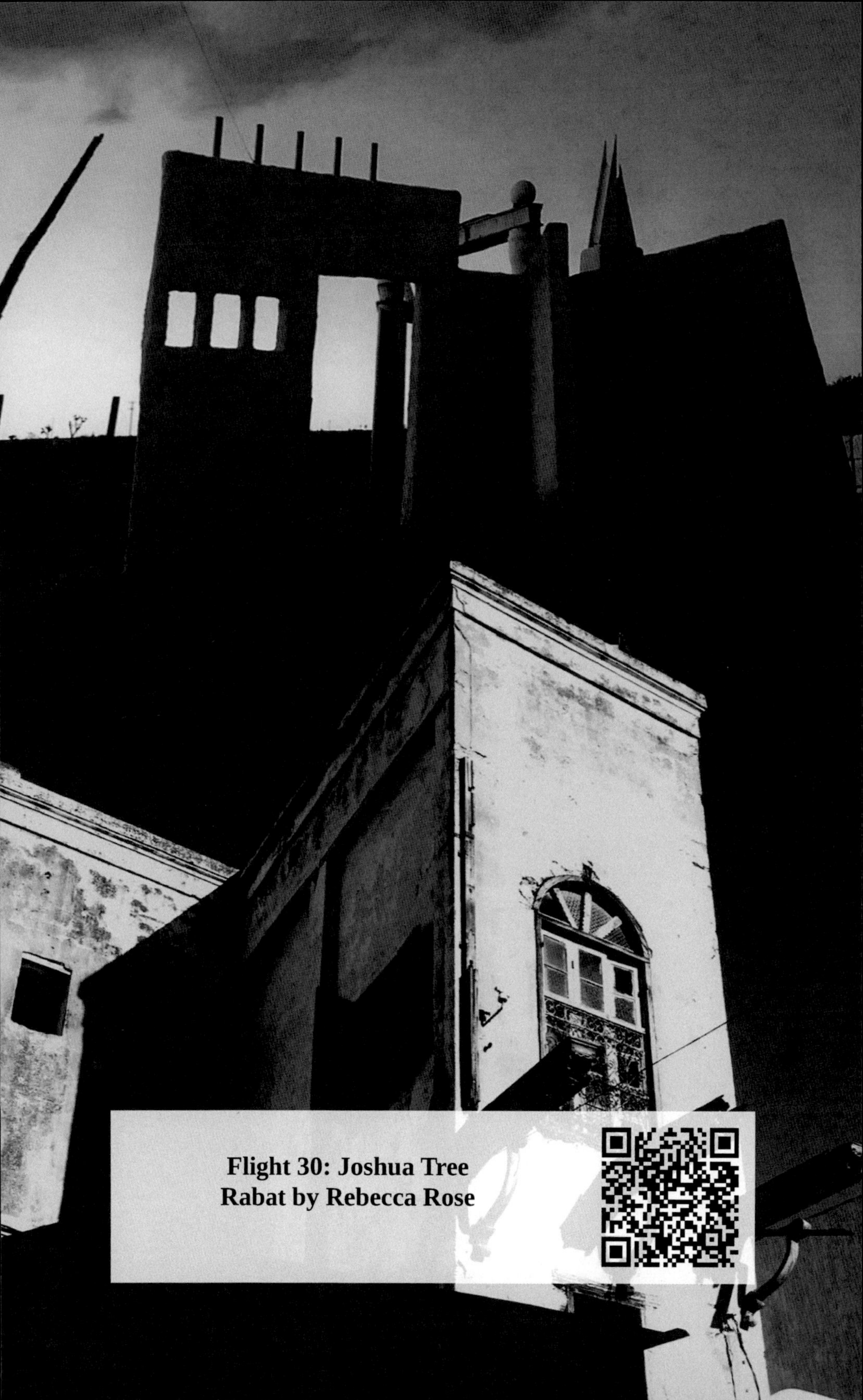
Flight 30: Joshua Tree
Rabat by Rebecca Rose

or participate in charitable auctions, the proceeds go directly to the designated cause, bypassing intermediaries and ensuring significant financial assistance with a global reach. This democratization of giving allows people from all around the world to participate in philanthropy, promoting inclusivity and broad support for charitable efforts. Moreover, NFTs can be designed to promote awareness of important social issues and charitable initiatives, sparking conversations and raising awareness among a wider audience. As unique incentives for donors, NFTs offer a dual benefit—donors gain the satisfaction of supporting a good cause while owning a valuable digital asset they can enjoy or potentially resell.

Artists and creators can dedicate a portion of their NFT sales royalties to charity, providing sustained support to causes over time. This ongoing contribution model ensures a lasting impact and continued financial aid for charities.

NFTs offer the potential to tokenize ownership of real-world assets, and the funds raised from these token sales can be channeled toward philanthropic causes, creating exciting new avenues for fundraising. Embracing NFTs in philanthropy also taps into the tech-savvy and digitally connected younger generation, motivating them to actively participate in making a positive impact on society.

Embracing NFTs for philanthropy demonstrates a forward-thinking and innovative approach to charitable giving. This can attract new donors and supporters who are excited about exploring novel ways to contribute to social causes.

My first foray into philanthropy within the NFT space occurred when Nadya Tolokonnikova launched a special NFT drop. The funds raised from this auction were dedicated to supporting the creation of activist art and aiding victims of domestic violence in Russia. In a significant moment for me, I successfully won that auction, contributing 100

ETH to the cause.

Subsequently, I participated in another philanthropic initiative called NFT4GOOD, which utilized its platform to raise funds for the #StopAsianHate movement. My Mondoir rookie card became part of this endeavor, and I was delighted to witness its success–as it sold over 100 pieces, generating the most funds for the cause.

Embracing the opportunity to make a difference, I've also participated in several other fundraising events within the NFT space, including supporting New York Cares through various initiatives. These experiences have allowed me to witness firsthand the transformative power of NFTs in driving positive change and supporting meaningful causes.

One of the most profound experiences on this philanthropic journey was my involvement with a UK-based charity project called Time to Help. This organization was dedicated to raising funds through NFTs to build water wells in the remote Kawulumu Village in Uganda. Recognizing the transformative potential of NFTs, I became the first donor, and the resulting well was named in my honor. This moment served as a powerful realization of the impact and potential of NFTs. It demonstrated that this new technology could go beyond creating art and accumulating wealth; it could change lives in tangible, meaningful ways.

Inspired by these experiences, I embarked on creating my own NFTs with the primary purpose of helping those in need. One of my earliest ventures was the creation of The NFT Guild, a collectible symbolizing a commitment to leveraging this emerging technology for the greater good. Available in three distinct editions, this piece resonated with the community and quickly sold out. This success further reinforced my belief in the power of NFTs as a catalyst for positive change.

I have actively participated in various philanthropic initiatives within the NFT space. I have minted and sold NFTs with the specific aim of supporting causes close to my heart. Whether it was aiding the families affected by the tragedy of Flight PS752, contributing to the Women Life Freedom movement in Iran, or participating in charity fundraising events, each NFT sold became a step toward making a difference.

Within my digital art collection, I proudly hold hundreds of pieces that serve as tangible evidence of my active involvement in a diverse array of philanthropic and charitable endeavors through NFTs. Each artwork represents my contributions to various causes, making a positive impact on the world.

From using NFTs to raise funds for animal shelters, lending support to victims of domestic abuse, those affected by earthquakes in Turkey, and those enduring the hardships of war in Ukraine, to backing educational initiatives, frontline workers during the COVID-19 pandemic, veterans, victims of child abuse, and countless other noble causes within the NFT space, I have found immense fulfillment in leveraging the power of this technology to make a meaningful difference in people's lives.

Collecting these pieces isn't just about the art; it's about the purpose behind each acquisition, symbolizing the unity between art and philanthropy and the profound impact this fusion can have on communities worldwide.

These experiences have solidified my belief in the potential of NFTs as a force for good. They not only provide artists with a medium for expressing their creativity but also become a catalyst for meaningful change in the world. By leveraging the power of NFTs for philanthropic endeavors, I aim to inspire others to join this movement and make a positive impact in their own unique ways.

Picture a world where every act of kindness or good deed you've ever performed in your life earned you a special sticker or badge, proudly showcasing your participation. Just imagine the impact that could have on inspiring your children, friends, and even strangers to follow in your footsteps and spread goodness in the world. Moreover, having these unique tokens as a beautiful reminder of each time you've offered a helping hand would be incredibly heartwarming and motivational.

Now, with the advent of NFTs, this concept has become a reality. NFTs allow us to create digital representations of these acts of kindness, memorializing them in a way that's secure, verifiable, and special. Each NFT becomes a symbol of the positive influence we've had in the world, and it serves as a beacon of encouragement for others to embrace compassion and generosity. With NFTs, we can capture the essence of our altruistic endeavors and use them to foster a more caring and thoughtful global community.

Facing Challenges

Throughout my journey in the NFT space, I have encountered my fair share of challenges. While the experience has been undeniably exciting and filled with opportunities, it has not always been smooth sailing.

At the beginning of my journey, I found myself navigating the ClubHouse platform—a space where I interacted with audiences from diverse cultures and backgrounds, in English (my second language). As someone born and raised in Iran, I lacked a deep understanding of international norms and the intricacies of communicating with a global audience, especially given the vast array of taboos and potentially offensive words that could be unintentionally used.

The pressure to expose myself and be vulnerable by speaking to large audiences was overwhelming, especially during my first time on a Clubhouse stage with around 2000 listeners. I felt the need to

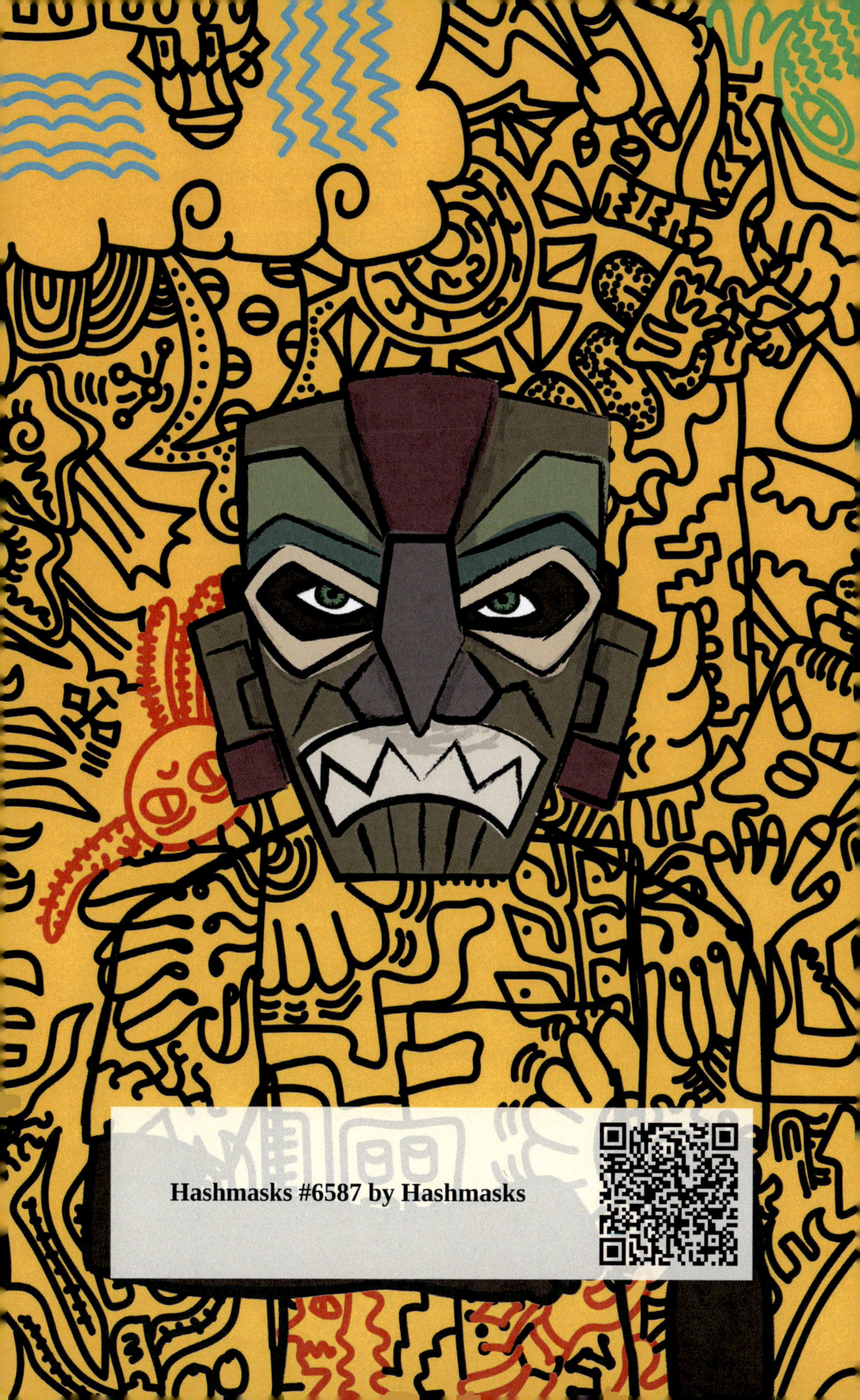
Hashmasks #6587 by Hashmasks

preface each of my speeches by explaining that English was not my primary language, offering apologies in case I used words incorrectly. Gradually, however, I gained enough confidence to embrace my linguistic challenges and speak with greater assurance. Nevertheless, even to this day, I find myself struggling with certain words, and my tongue is not fully accustomed to pronouncing them correctly.

One of the most treasured aspects of the NFT community is the collective understanding and acceptance of its international nature. It is widely acknowledged that not everyone speaks English as their native tongue, and this inclusivity fosters an environment where language barriers are not seen as impediments but rather as unique and celebrated aspects of each individual's journey.

Throughout my time in the NFT space, I have never encountered any criticism or negativity regarding my English proficiency. This speaks volumes about the supportive and compassionate nature of the community, where individuals are encouraged to share their stories, experiences, and perspectives regardless of language challenges.

Starting my journey in the NFT space presented a significant challenge, but it also became a testament to the power of acceptance, understanding, and genuine connection within an international community of diverse voices. The platform has given me the opportunity to grow as a communicator and learn from others around the world, proving that unity and shared experiences can transcend language barriers and create a space where everyone's voice is valued and heard.

During the early days of my journey, I encountered a unique challenge within my fellow Iranian community. Some individuals accused me of owning NFT art platforms and manipulating them to draw interest and financial gain from my fellow Iranians. They even went as far as accusing me of seeking to position myself as a leader, using

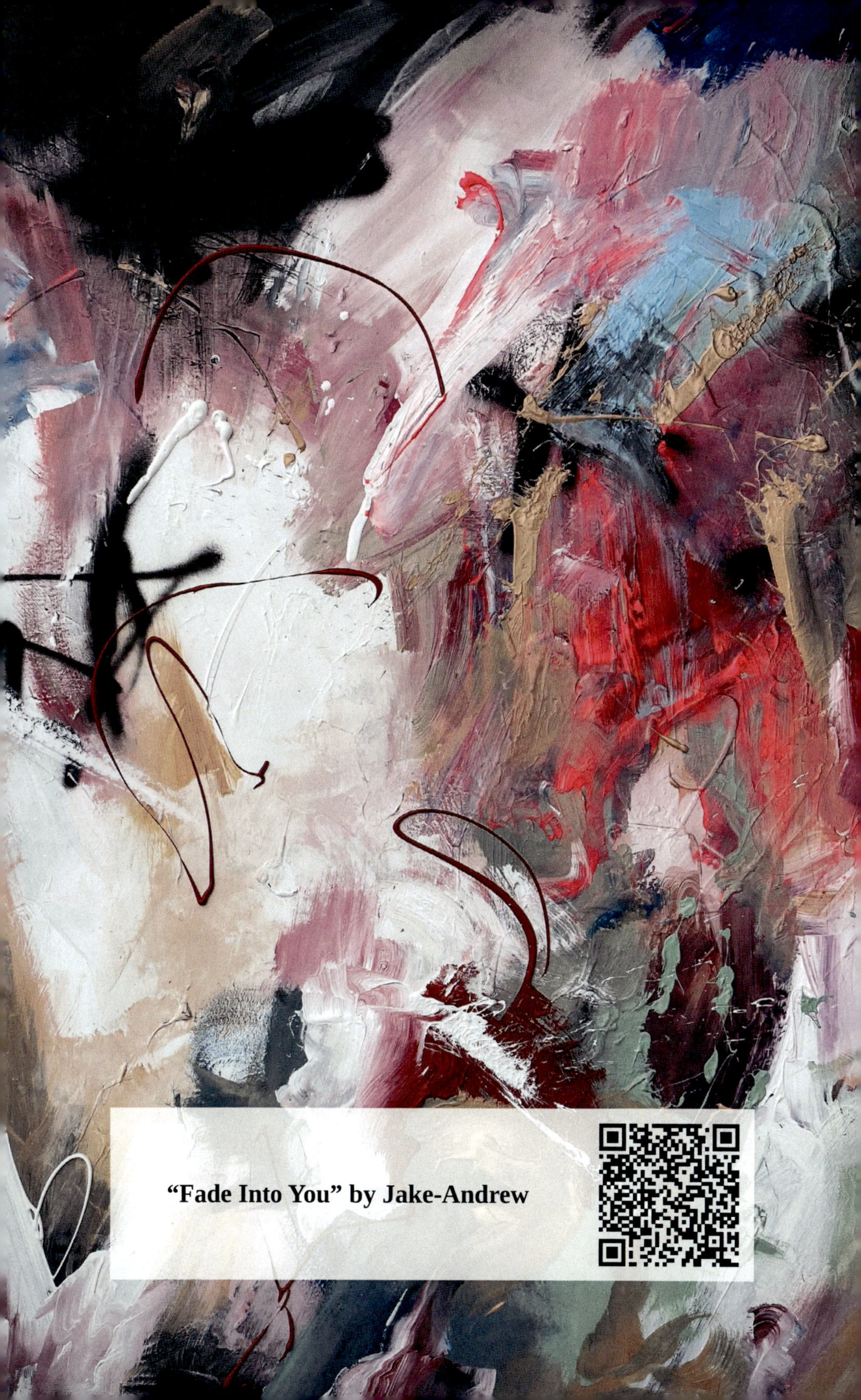
"Fade Into You" by Jake-Andrew

this platform to exert influence over Iranians in political and social domains. Comparisons were drawn to Ayatollah Khomeini, and I found myself facing public criticism for supposedly trying to become a "supreme leader."

In many communities, the term "community leader" or "thought leader" is a common label for those who play a significant role within the community. However, when such labels were associated with me, my fellow Iranians reacted with sharp criticism and skepticism. It took time for them to understand that my intentions were far more profound than seeking leadership status. My true agenda was driven by genuine love and dedication to art and technology, as well as a deep desire to contribute to the betterment of the NFT community.

Over time, I was able to communicate my true intentions and motivations to my fellow Iranians. I wanted to foster a community that celebrated art, technology, and creativity and to use the NFT space as a means of creating a positive impact and unity within the community. Gradually, they came to realize that my involvement in the NFT world was fueled by a sincere passion for art and technology, not by a quest for power or influence.

Another significant challenge I faced was the constant pressure from artists to purchase their work. As my collection grew, I found myself inundated with messages and offers from artists, each hoping to secure a sale. It was overwhelming at times, as I realized that many artists saw collectors solely as potential buyers rather than building genuine connections or appreciating the art itself.

At a certain point, I experienced a profound mental breakdown, struggling internally with conflicting emotions. On the one hand, I was deeply committed to this space and passionate about contributing to the building of this new era. However, I was disheartened by the fact that artists seemed to view me solely as a source of financial support rather than recognizing my genuine conviction and love for the NFT space.

The realization that artists only reached out to me when they had a piece for sale or an auction running left me feeling disappointed and hurt. This emotional turmoil led me to step away from the NFT space for a period of four weeks to confront and address this internal conflict.

During this time, something unexpected happened. Several artists, including Rebecca Rose, from whom I had never acquired a piece–sent messages to check on my well-being. Rebecca Rose's message, in particular, touched my heart deeply. In a single act of kindness and genuine concern, she asked about my mental health, proving that there was a sense of humanity and care within the NFT community.

Receiving this message from Rebecca Rose was a turning point for me. It reminded me of the authentic connections that could exist within the NFT space and reignited my determination to prove my worth beyond being perceived merely as a financial supporter. I realized that I am more than just a purse; I am a passionate advocate, a believer in the transformative power of NFTs, and someone who genuinely cares about the well-being of artists and the community.

With renewed strength and conviction, I decided to return to the NFT space and continue my journey, fighting to make a difference and demonstrate that my involvement goes far beyond monetary contributions. This experience reminded me of the importance of genuine connections and the profound impact a simple act of kindness can have on someone's life.

I had the privilege of connecting with artists who truly valued meaningful connections and appreciated the essence of their craft. They recognized that the NFT space was about more than just financial gain; it was about building a supportive community and fostering

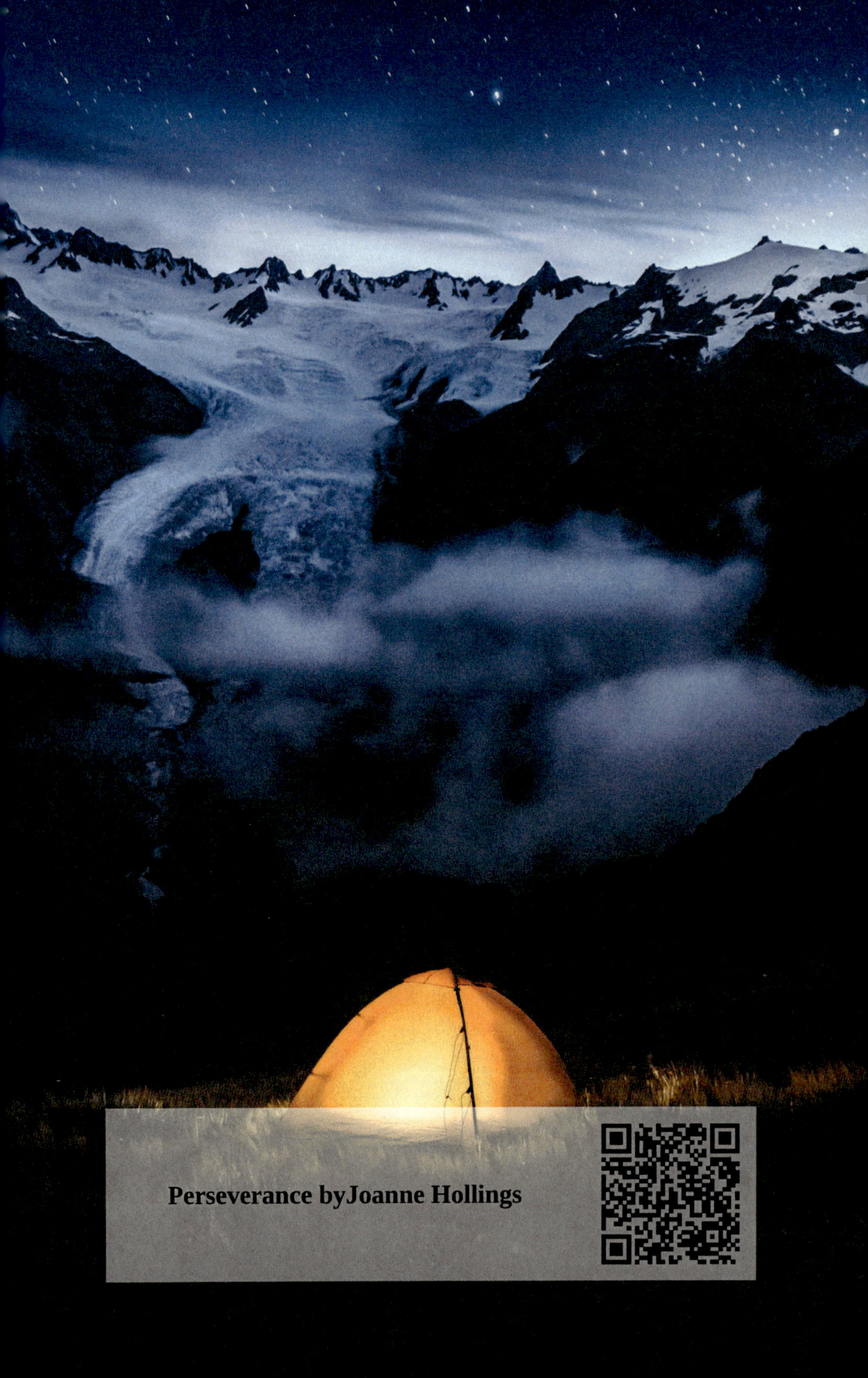

Perseverance byJoanne Hollings

artistic expression. These artists understood that the true value of art lay in its ability to evoke emotions, communicate ideas, and inspire change.

Reflecting on these experiences, I realized the importance of staying true to my passion for art and fostering genuine connections within the community. It became clear that collecting should always be driven by a love for the art itself rather than solely focusing on potential returns or succumbing to market trends. While financial aspects have their place, they should always uphold the core values of art appreciation and meaningful connections.

I prioritize art and connection above all else. By valuing an artist's unique vision, investing in personal relationships, and supporting emerging talents, collectors can create a more authentic and fulfilling experience. This philosophy not only benefits the artists and the community at large, but it also helps to foster a stronger, more sustainable NFT ecosystem.

One of the most significant and profound challenges in my journey as an NFT collector was when my all-time favorite artist, DeeKay, put a piece up for auction. This artwork held immense importance for several reasons. DeeKay had initiated a project called "Let's Walk" two years prior, and I was one of the first collectors to acquire his very first drop for this collection. The piece that was going to auction served as the grand finale of the Let's Walk series, making it an especially meaningful moment for me to show my unwavering support for the artist's artistic journey.

During this time, my financial situation was dire, as I was planning to relocate to Dubai to establish my gallery there. The imminent move entailed significant expenses, and on top of it all, the auction day had arrived. Driven by an overwhelming desire to own this special artwork, I started bidding with fierce determination. My mind was set on winning this piece, regardless of the challenges ahead.

When the auction concluded, I emerged as the victorious bidder. However, in order to fund my purchase, I had to make a difficult decision. I chose to sell one of the wristwatches my wife had given me as a birthday gift. Without hesitation, I parted with the cherished gift and promptly sent the money to the auction house to secure DeeKay's artwork.

In a heartwarming gesture, DeeKay reached out to me, offering financial support to cover the cost of the artwork. This act of kindness spoke volumes about the character of the artist and the connection we shared.

Even though the watch's sale was initially meant to fund our move to Dubai, I chose to channel the funds to support my dear friend and one of the most significant artists I have come to know. It was an act of deep conviction and love for the art, culture, and vibrant NFT community. Despite the financial challenges and uncertainties, my unwavering belief in the values of Web3 and the power of artistic expression drove me to make this profound choice.

In retrospect, it is not a matter of conviction or stupidity. Rather, it was a manifestation of my genuine passion for art and my commitment to supporting artists who make a difference in the world through their creative contributions. It symbolized my dedication to the NFT space and its ethos, emphasizing the profound impact that art and community can have on one's life and choices.

One pressing challenge that impacts not only me but also the entire NFT art and collectible community is the presence of creators with questionable intentions. Some well-known artists view NFTs as an opportunity to exploit the system solely for financial gain, creating an atmosphere of mistrust and disillusionment among collectors and the general public alike.

This troubling trend has given rise to a bubble of disheartening experiences. The misguided actions of certain creators have resulted in a loss of authenticity and integrity within the NFT space. Regrettably, some individuals with dishonest intentions are capitalizing on the popularity of NFTs to deceive and defraud unsuspecting collectors.

The crypto culture, unfortunately, has also attracted scammers who manipulate NFT collectible drops, causing many to suffer financial losses. These fraudulent activities not only tarnish the reputation of genuine creators and the NFT ecosystem but also create hesitancy and apprehension among potential collectors.

Addressing this issue is crucial for the sustainability and growth of the NFT community. By promoting transparency, educating collectors about potential risks, and actively weeding out scammers, we can work collectively to foster a safer and more trustworthy environment for all participants in the NFT space. Ensuring that NFTs continue to be valued for their artistic merit and unique properties is essential in preserving the true spirit of creativity and innovation that defines this revolutionary art form.

Another pressing challenge that extends beyond the NFT space is the prevalence of cancel culture. Within this creative realm, there have been numerous instances where creators and builders have been subjected to harsh targeting, severe criticism, and unwarranted attacks, ultimately leading to their cancellation. Regrettably, this trend is not unique to the NFT community, as cancel culture has pervaded various aspects of modern society.

In this space, most individuals often find themselves influenced by a vocal minority wielding significant control and power, primarily motivated by their own financial interests. These individuals freely

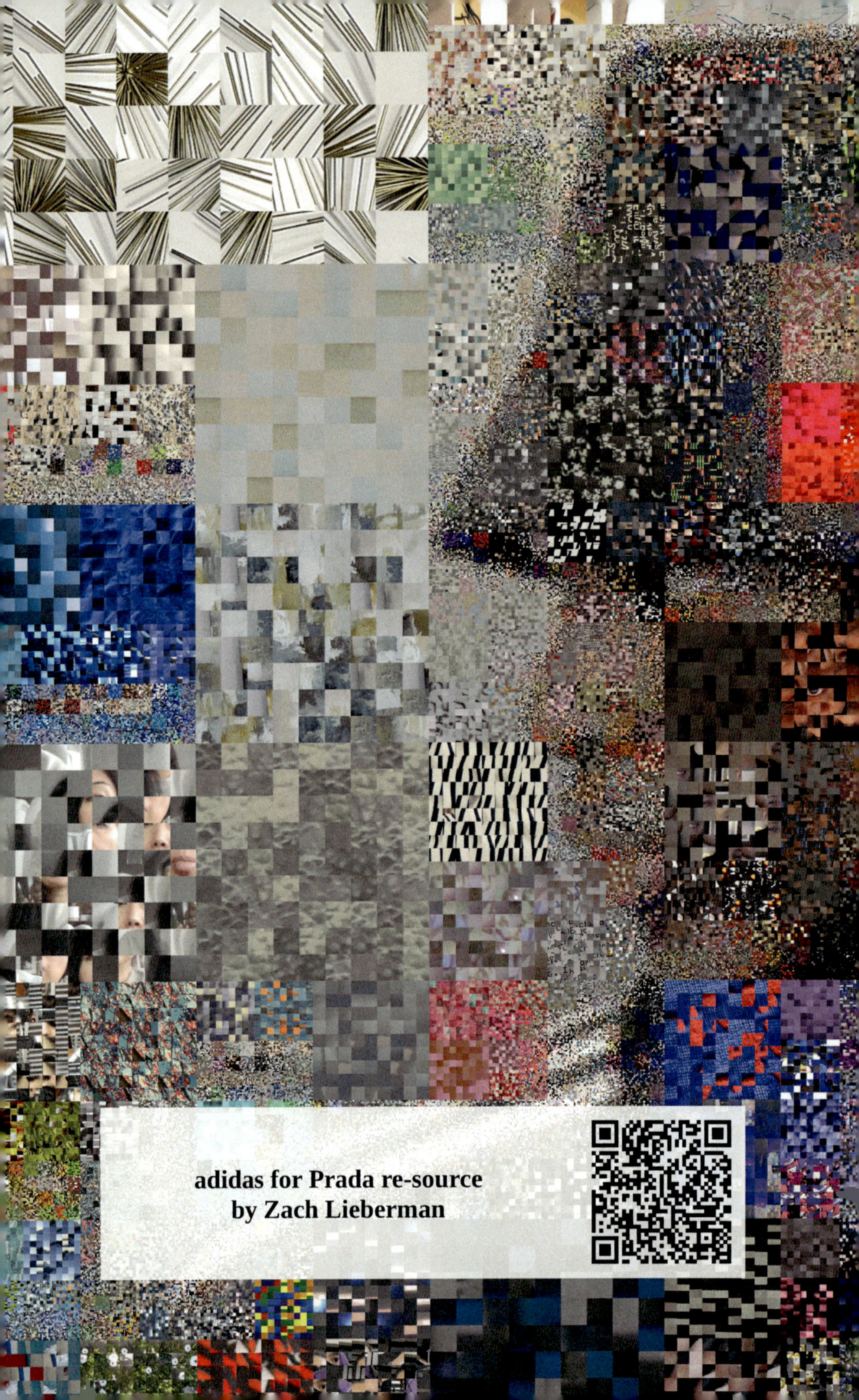
adidas for Prada re-source
by Zach Lieberman

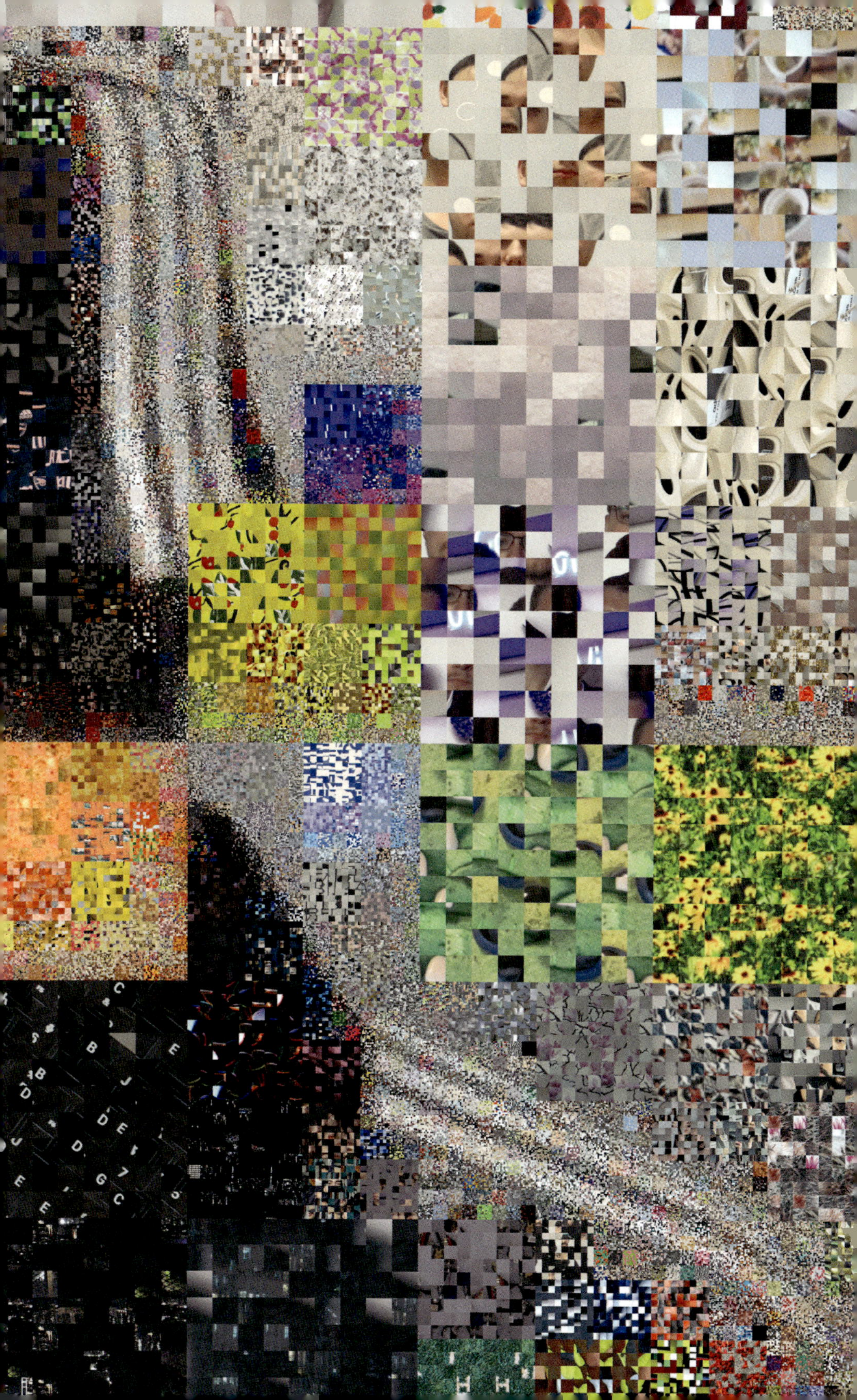

cancel those they perceive as potential threats without taking the time to delve deeper into the underlying issues, seeking to understand them, or assuming positive intent. Instead of engaging in constructive dialogue, they merely follow the trend of canceling others without considering the consequences of their actions.

The impact of cancel culture on creators and builders in the NFT market has been profound. Many talented individuals have been forced to leave the space, feeling disheartened and frustrated by the unwarranted attacks and the lack of empathy and support from the community.

Addressing this challenge requires fostering a culture of open-mindedness, empathy, and constructive criticism. Encouraging thoughtful discussions and understanding diverse perspectives can pave the way for a more inclusive and supportive environment within the NFT space and beyond. Recognizing that cancel culture can be detrimental to creativity and innovation, we must work together to create an atmosphere where creators and builders feel safe and empowered to express their ideas and contribute to the growth of the NFT community.

During my 20s, I was a well-known basketball player and somewhat of a celebrity in Iran, standing tall at 6’7”. Whether due to my status in Iran or my towering height, I always seemed to draw attention wherever I went. This constant visibility instilled a sense of self-confidence in me, as I never had to actively seek recognition or try to be noticed. It was a familiar sensation. As a result, I remained humble and never sought to take advantage of my status in any situation.

In the NFT space, this confidence translated into not feeling the need to show off or use my status to gain attention or advantage over others. I have always been outspoken and never sought approval from anyone, which presented its challenges in a space where many tend to follow those who make the loudest noise, create controversy, or seek attention through ostentatious displays.

Despite this, I remained true to myself and stayed focused on engaging with the community in a meaningful way rather than seeking superficial attention. My approach may not have been the most flashy, but I believe in the power of wisdom and meaningful connections over empty noise. As a result, my outreach and engagement may have remained more low-key, but it has always been genuine and authentic.

The challenges I have encountered along my journey serve as reminders to remain grounded and true to my beliefs as a collector. They reinforced the importance of seeking out artists who share a genuine passion for their craft and fostering connections that go beyond mere transactions. By sharing this advice, I hope to inspire others to approach their own collecting journey with a similar mindset, placing art and connection at the forefront and embracing the transformative power of the NFT community.

Collectibles vs. Art

Art and collectibles have played essential roles in human history and culture, each with its own distinct origins and significance. The creation of art predates recorded history, with early humans expressing their experiences and beliefs through cave paintings and rock carvings tens of thousands of years ago. These ancient artworks, such as the cave paintings in Lascaux and Altamira, provide glimpses into the creative expressions of our ancestors, showcasing their desire to communicate and leave a mark on the world.

On the other hand, the concept of collectibles emerged later in human history. The first known collectible items appeared in the ancient world, where individuals began to value and preserve objects for their rarity, aesthetic appeal, or historical importance. These collectibles could include ancient coins, precious stones, and artifacts of cultural significance.

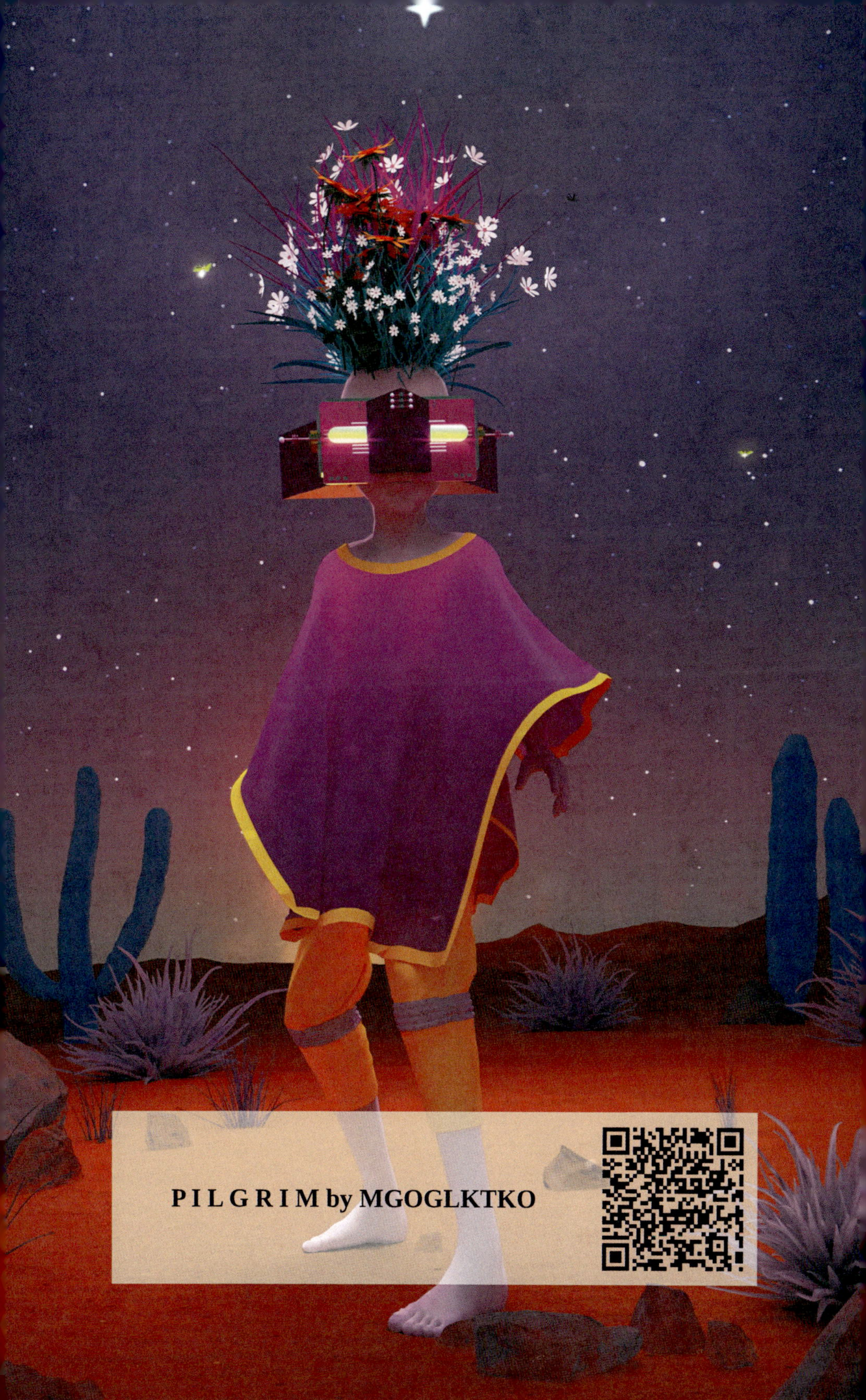
PILGRIM by MGOGLKTKO

Throughout the ages, both art and collectibles continued to evolve, reflecting the changing tastes and values of different civilizations. Art transformed from cave paintings and sculptures to encompass various mediums and styles, from Renaissance paintings to modern digital art. Collectibles, too, expanded to include a wide range of objects, from antique coins and stamps to sports memorabilia and trading cards.

The key difference between art and collectibles lies in their primary purpose and value. Art is primarily a form of creative expression, allowing artists to convey emotions, tell stories, and reflect on the world around them. It holds intrinsic value as an expression of human creativity and has profound cultural and emotional significance.

On the other hand, collectibles are valued more for their rarity, historical importance, or connection to specific events or individuals. Collectors often seek these items for their uniqueness or as a means of preserving a piece of history.

While art and collectibles may sometimes overlap, they serve distinct purposes and appeal to different aspects of human fascination. Art speaks to our creative souls, while collectibles speak to our curiosity about the past and our desire to preserve tangible pieces of history. Both art and collectibles enrich our lives, offering unique insights into the human experience and our ever-evolving journey through time.

In the digital age, art and collectibles have taken on new dimensions through the emergence of NFTs. NFTs have revolutionized the way we perceive, own, and trade both art and collectibles in the digital realm. While both can exist as NFTs, there are essential distinctions between the two.

NFT art represents digital artworks that are uniquely tokenized on the blockchain. These digital creations encompass a broad spectrum of artistic expressions, ranging from digital paintings, illustrations, and animations to virtual reality experiences and interactive installations. NFT art allows artists to showcase their creativity in a digital space, providing a secure and transparent way to prove ownership and authenticity. As NFTs, digital art gains provable scarcity and immutability, making NFTs desirable collectibles for art enthusiasts and investors alike.

NFT collectibles, on the other hand, encompass a diverse array of digital assets that are unique and scarce digital assets. These can include virtual trading cards, digital toys, in-game assets, and more. Unlike NFT art, which is typically a standalone piece, NFT collectibles often belong to a series or set, each with its distinct attributes and rarity levels. They cater to the human desire to own something limited and valuable, similar to traditional collectibles like rare coins or trading cards. NFT collectibles have gained immense popularity, especially in the realm of blockchain-based gaming and virtual worlds, where players can collect, trade, and interact with these digital assets.

While both art and collectibles can be represented as NFTs, their primary distinctions lie in their purpose and value. NFT art's primary objective is to serve as an artistic expression, provoking emotions and telling stories through digital means. The value of NFT art often lies in its artistic merit and the reputation of the creator.

NFT collectibles, on the other hand, are valued for their rarity, uniqueness, and the significance they hold within a collection or series. Some NFT collectibles gain value due to their connection to popular franchises or collaborations with well-known brands and artists.

While both NFT art and NFT collectibles share the underlying technology of blockchain and tokenization, they cater to different aspects of human fascination. NFT art appeals to our appreciation for creativity and aesthetics, while NFT collectibles fulfill our desire to own and collect unique, scarce digital assets. Together, they form an exciting and transformative ecosystem within the world of NFTs, opening up new possibilities for artists, collectors, and enthusiasts in the digital era.

As a collector, I place value on both collectibles and art, and my collection includes a wide range of known NFT collectibles, such as CryptoPunks and Bored Ape Yacht Club. However, I find that collecting digital art holds a different and profound meaning for me. While acquiring a collectible may provide a sense of belonging to a specific group or social class, similar to how purchasing a luxury brand item distinguishes you from others, collecting art carries a deeper significance.

Art, in its essence, bestows upon the collector a sense of patronage, a profound appreciation, and an opportunity to learn and grow. Each artwork I collect becomes a vessel for wisdom, knowledge, and new perspectives. Unlike collectibles, which might only offer a sense of community belonging or, at best, a financial gain for fortunate collectors, art enriches my life with a deeper understanding of the human experience, diverse cultures, and the artists' unique visions.

Through collecting digital art, I engage in a journey of exploration, delving into the thoughts and emotions of the artists and connecting with the stories they tell through their creations. The act of acquiring art transcends mere ownership; it becomes an exchange of creative energy between the artist and the collector, fostering a bond that extends beyond material possessions.

Each piece of art I collect becomes a part of my personal narrative, contributing to my growth as an individual and expanding my horizons. The artistic expressions I collect become cherished treasures, representing moments of artistic brilliance and inspiration.

While collectibles hold their appeal, it is the world of art that captivates my heart and soul. The beauty of collecting digital art lies in the endless possibilities it presents—possibilities to be moved, to be enlightened, and to be transformed through the transformative power of art.

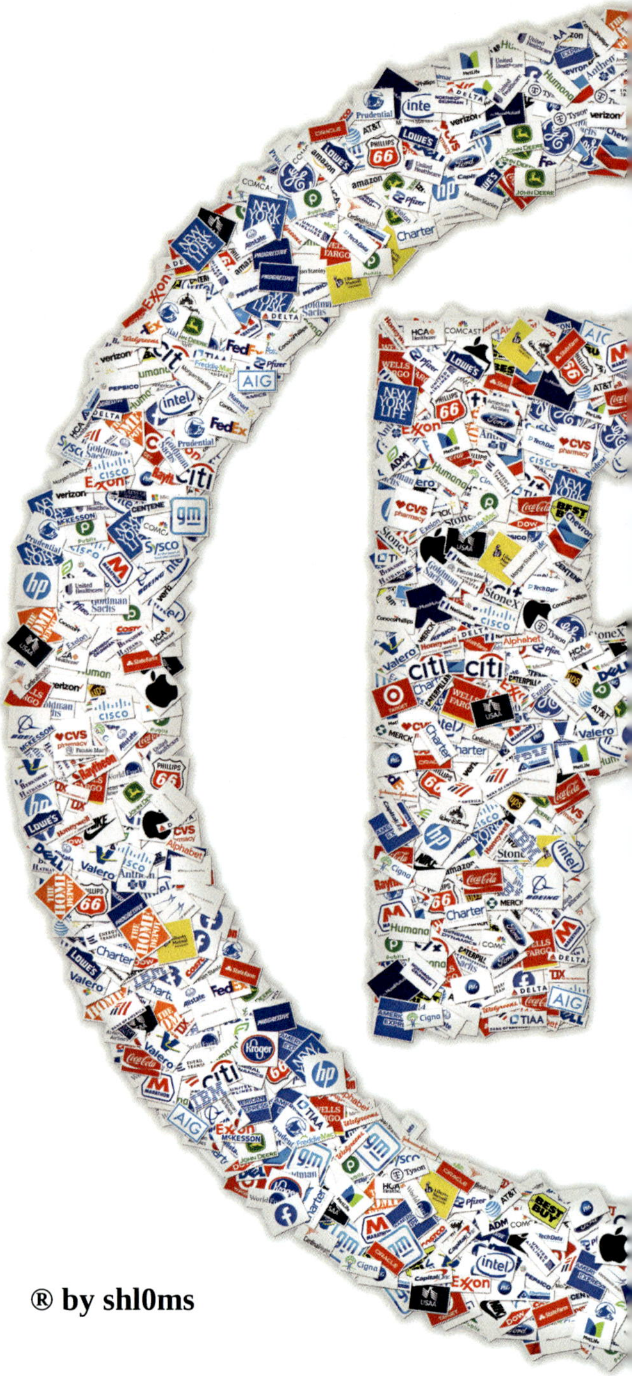

® by shl0ms

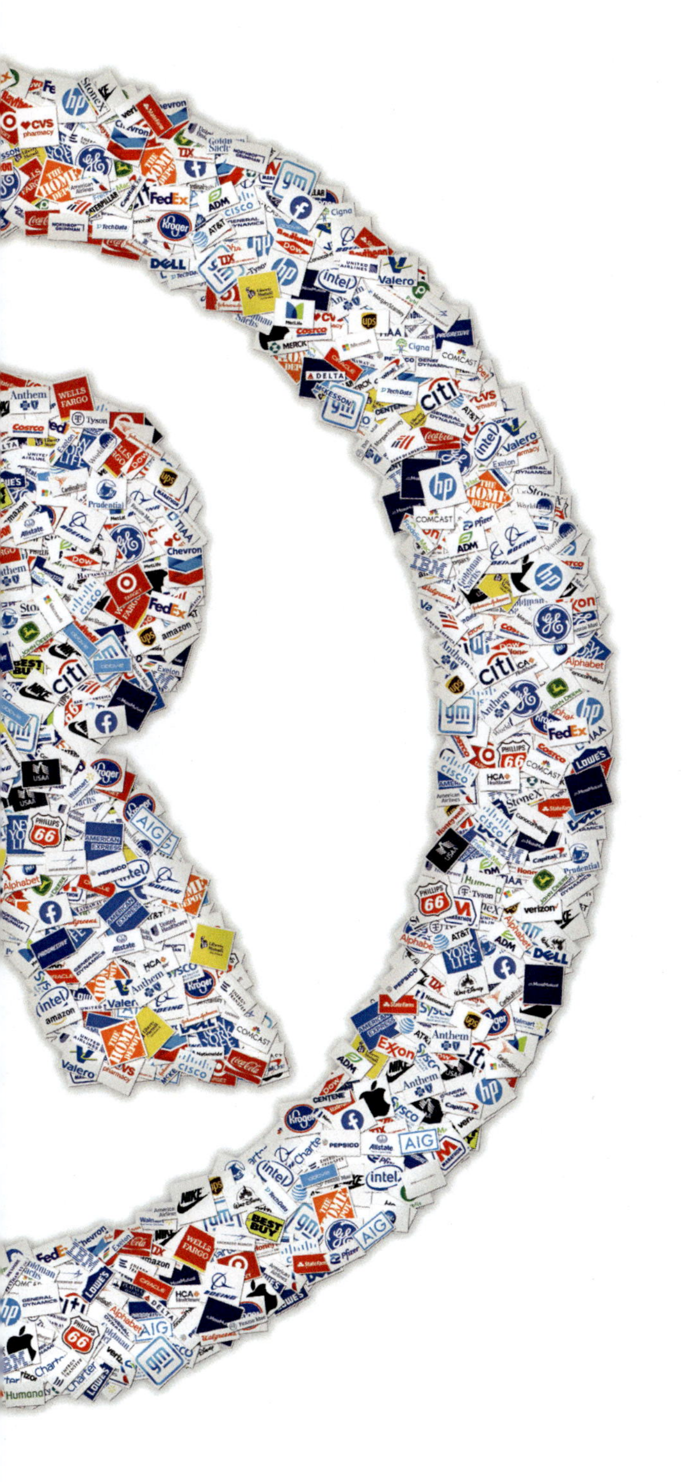

Collecting Philosophy

People collect art for many reasons, and the motivations behind art collecting can be deeply personal and varied.

Many art collectors are drawn to the beauty and visual appeal of artworks. They derive pleasure and satisfaction from surrounding themselves with pieces that resonate with their tastes and aesthetics. Collecting art allows them to curate a space that reflects their unique sense of beauty.

Art has the power to evoke emotions, memories, and feelings in a profound way. Collectors often choose artworks that hold personal significance or resonate with their life experiences. The emotional connection to art can make the collection deeply meaningful and a reflection of the collector's journey.

Art can also be viewed as a financial investment. Some collectors see art as a store of value that may appreciate over time. They may invest in emerging artists whose works they believe will gain value in the future. However, it is essential to note that art investment can be speculative and is not guaranteed to yield high returns.

Art can be intellectually stimulating, challenging our perceptions and expanding our understanding of the world. Collectors who appreciate thought-provoking and conceptually rich artworks are motivated by the intellectual engagement that art offers.

Owning valuable artworks, especially those by renowned artists, can confer social status and prestige. Art collections can be a symbol of cultural sophistication and success, making them attractive to some collectors.

Many collectors are passionate about supporting artists and the art community. By purchasing and collecting art, they provide artists with financial support and recognition, helping them sustain their creative practices.

Art collecting allows individuals to create narratives and stories through their collections. Each artwork becomes a piece of a larger puzzle, contributing to the collector's unique narrative and perspective on art and culture.

Engaging with art can be a journey of self-discovery and personal growth. Collectors may find themselves exploring new art movements, cultures, and ideas, broadening their horizons and enriching their understanding of the world.

Art-collecting philosophy encompasses the principles and beliefs that guide a collector's approach to acquiring and curating artworks. It goes beyond simply amassing valuable pieces and delves into the deeper meaning and purpose behind building an art collection. It is highly individual and can vary significantly from one collector to another, influenced by personal experiences, tastes, and values.

At its core, art-collecting philosophy revolves around passion and genuine appreciation for art. It starts with a love for the creative process and the desire to support artists in their artistic journey. Collectors with a strong art-collecting philosophy prioritize the emotional and intellectual connection they have with a piece over its potential financial value. They see their collection as a reflection of their identity and values, and each artwork tells a story of the collector's artistic journey.

Art collectors who embrace a philosophical approach often seek out artworks that align with their beliefs and personal narratives. They look for pieces that provoke thought, evoke emotions, and communicate ideas that resonate with them. Authenticity is a key aspect of their selection process, as they are drawn to artists who remain true to their unique style and vision, creating works that stand the test of time.

Building a collection with a philosophical foundation is not solely about the individual artworks; it's also about the relationships and connections formed within the artistic community. These collectors actively engage with artists, curators, and fellow collectors, fostering a sense of community and camaraderie. These collectors understand that art is not created in isolation but is interconnected with the cultural, social, and historical context of its time.

Additionally, art-collecting philosophy can encompass philanthropy and social responsibility. Many collectors use their passion for art as a means to support artists, art institutions, and charitable causes. They may actively participate in charity auctions, fund art education programs, or donate artworks to public collections.

Ultimately, art collecting philosophy is an ever-evolving journey. It reflects the growth and transformation of the collector as they continue to explore the world of art. It is an expression of their individuality, values, and aspirations, shaping a unique and meaningful collection that has a profound impact on their life and the broader artistic community.

My initial attraction to artworks was primarily based on their aesthetic appeal. The look and feel of a piece played a significant role in capturing my attention and piquing my interest. I was drawn to the visual impact and emotional response that art evoked within me. However, as I delved deeper into the world of NFTs and expanded my collection, my approach to art selection evolved, shaped by my experiences and the insights gained along my journey.

I began appreciating the importance of artists who remain true to their unique style and artistic vision. While trends may come and go, I realized that artists who stay authentic and committed to their artistic identities create a lasting impact. I started to appreciate their dedication to their craft, their exploration of their personal artistic language, and their ability to create a distinctive body of work that stood the test of time.

In this journey of exploration, I came to understand that the art of selection extended far beyond mere investment or trend-chasing. It was an intricate dance between the heart and the mind as I sought to build a collection that spoke to the core of my being. I envisioned a collection that transcended superficiality and instead reflected a cohesive narrative, a tapestry of artistic journeys woven together in harmony. I became more discerning in my choices. I realized that it was not merely about acquiring artworks that were popular or hyped up at a given moment. Instead, I sought out artists who demonstrated consistency in their artistic expression and a depth of creativity that resonated with me on a deeper level. I valued artworks that showcased the artist's individuality, their ability to convey emotion, and their

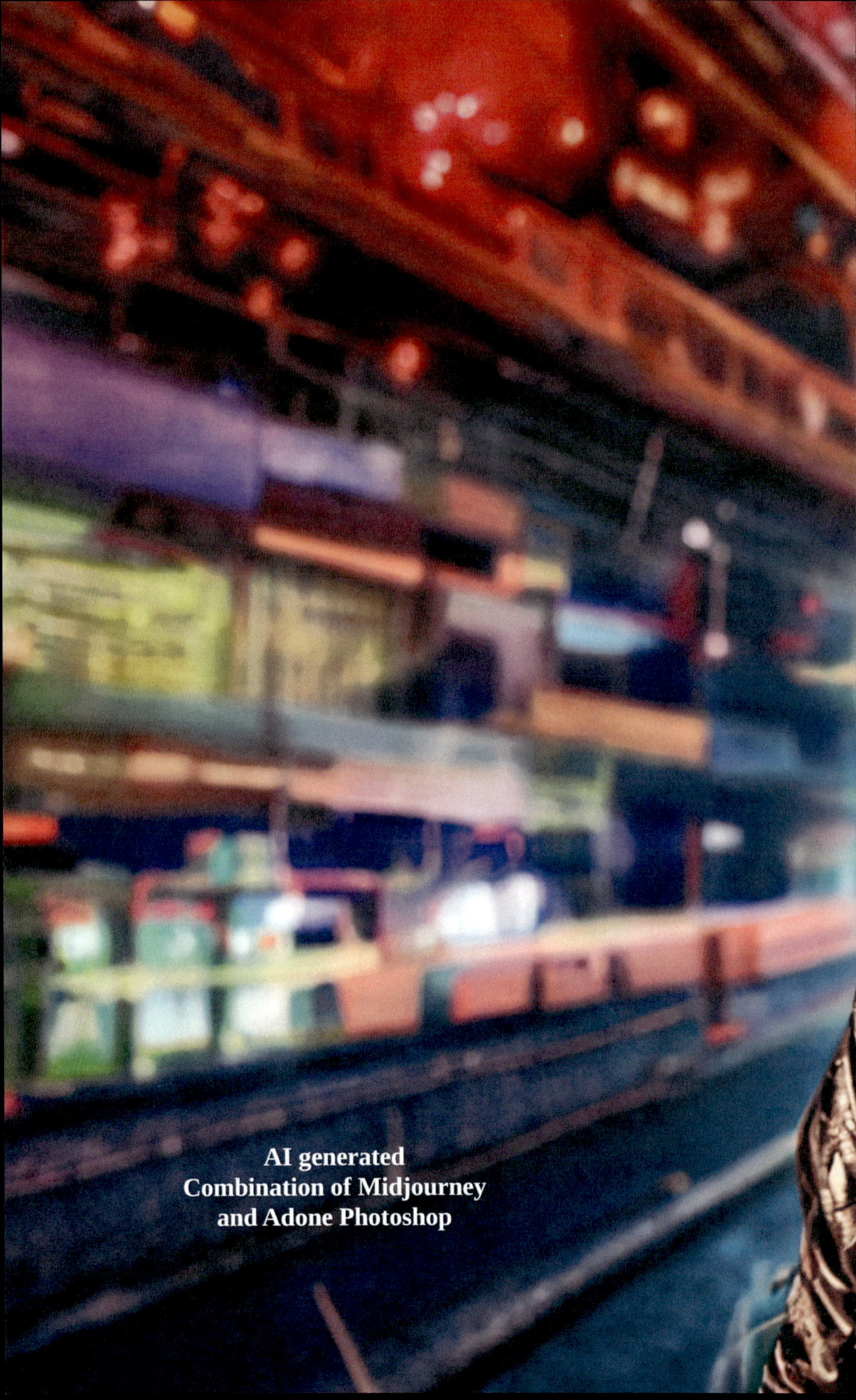

AI generated
Combination of Midjourney
and Adone Photoshop

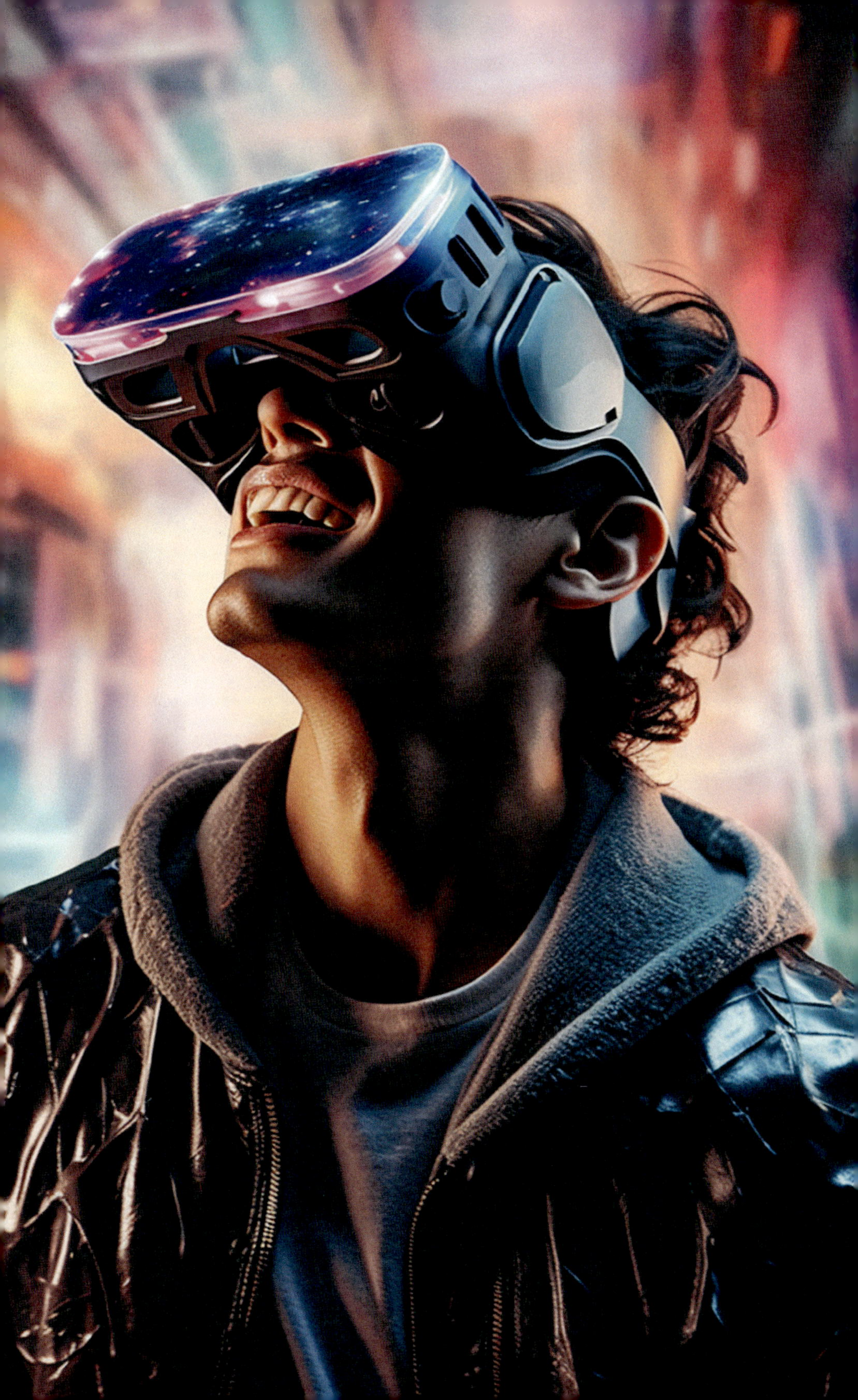

capacity to provoke thought and inspire.

By focusing on artists who stayed true to their unique style and artistic voice, I aimed to build a collection that reflected a cohesive narrative and conveyed a sense of authenticity. I believed in the power of art to tell stories and share ideas, and I wanted my collection to reflect the journeys and contributions of the artists behind each piece. It was about celebrating their artistic growth and supporting their development as creators.

Evolving as a Collector

As an art collector, my journey has been a path of continuous growth and exploration. When I first entered the world of art collecting, I was captivated by the sheer beauty and emotional resonance of artworks. The way they spoke to my soul and stirred my imagination inspired me to delve deeper into this passionate pursuit.

As my knowledge of the art world expanded, I became more discerning in my choices. I invested time in learning about different art movements, studying the stories behind the artworks, and engaging with artists to gain insights into their creative process. This deeper understanding enriched my collecting experience, allowing me to appreciate the nuances and intentions behind each piece.

One of the most rewarding aspects of my journey has been the relationships I forged with artists. Connecting with these talented individuals has given me a glimpse into their artistic vision and passion for their craft. These connections became an integral part of my collecting philosophy as I realized the profound impact of supporting emerging talents and giving them a platform to share their stories with the world.

While traditional art continues to hold a special place in my heart, I have embraced technological advancements in the art world with equal enthusiasm. NFTs and digital art offer exciting opportunities to explore new realms of creativity and ownership, reshaping the landscape of art collecting in unprecedented ways. My approach to collecting NFTs underwent a significant transformation. I became more deliberate and thoughtful about the pieces I chose to add to my collection, recognizing that each acquisition had the potential to contribute to a larger narrative and create value for lesser-known artists.

Rather than simply amassing a random assortment of artworks, I started to curate my collection with a purpose. I sought to create narratives and connections between the pieces, weaving together a cohesive story that showcased the diversity of artistic voices and styles within the NFT community. This approach allowed me to elevate the works of lesser-known artists, giving them a platform and recognition alongside more established creators.

In addition to curating my collection, I turned my attention toward building tools to address prevalent issues in the NFT space. I recognized the need for improved discovery mechanisms that would aid both collectors and artists in navigating the ever-expanding realm of digital art. I focused on creating tools that would facilitate the exploration of new artists, enhance accessibility, and foster connections within the community. By providing these solutions, I aimed to contribute to a more inclusive and supportive ecosystem for artists and collectors alike.

As my collection evolved, so did my desire to give back to the art community that had enriched my life so profoundly. I sought to support art education initiatives, champion charitable causes, and contribute to programs that fostered the growth of artists and art enthusiasts alike.

This evolution as a collector reflects my dedication to not only the growth of my personal collection but also to the advancement of the NFT space as a whole. By being intentional about the pieces I acquire and actively working toward solving challenges, I hope to make a meaningful impact on the community and support the continued development and adoption of NFTs. This journey is not just about personal collecting; it is about fostering a thriving and inclusive space for artists, collectors, and enthusiasts.

The Myth of Decentralization

Decentralization lies at the heart of blockchain technology, but in reality, achieving true decentralization remains a challenge, especially in today's landscape.

With Ethereum, the issue of centralization is a growing concern. Many users rely on centralized wallets to access the supposedly decentralized world of blockchains. The control exerted by centralized entities over node providers, platforms, and marketplaces, raises important questions about true decentralization.

Moreover, the influence wielded by a handful of centralized influencers over traders and flippers further undermines the claim of true decentralization. This influence can significantly impact market dynamics and user behavior within the space.

To add to the complexity, some participants in the blockchain ecosystem choose to remain anonymous, which can be seen as an attempt to protect themselves from potential centralized control and surveillance.

In an ideal decentralized system, access to the blockchain should also be decentralized, allowing the community to operate nodes and develop tools collectively. However, this remains challenging as many participants are focused on profit-making activities or are reliant on centralized sources of funding and support.

While the goal of achieving true decentralization is still a work in progress, awareness of the challenges and a commitment to address them are essential for fostering a more genuinely decentralized blockchain ecosystem. The community must strive to overcome the existing centralization bottlenecks and work toward a future where decentralization becomes more than just a claim but a reality in the blockchain space.

Despite the proliferation of tools aimed at democratizing access to the blockchain, the reality is that many of these tools are heavily influenced or backed by venture capitalists and centralized institutions. Unfortunately, projects that are bootstrapped and driven by individuals or smaller groups often struggle to gain recognition and support from the broader community.

In this so-called decentralized space, a significant number of projects and platforms are either owned or financially supported by VCs. This raises concerns about the true nature of decentralization and the potential influence of centralized entities on the direction and governance of these projects.

Moreover, achieving a completely decentralized ecosystem in today's society remains a significant challenge. Many people are not yet ready to fully embrace the principles of decentralization, and their behaviors

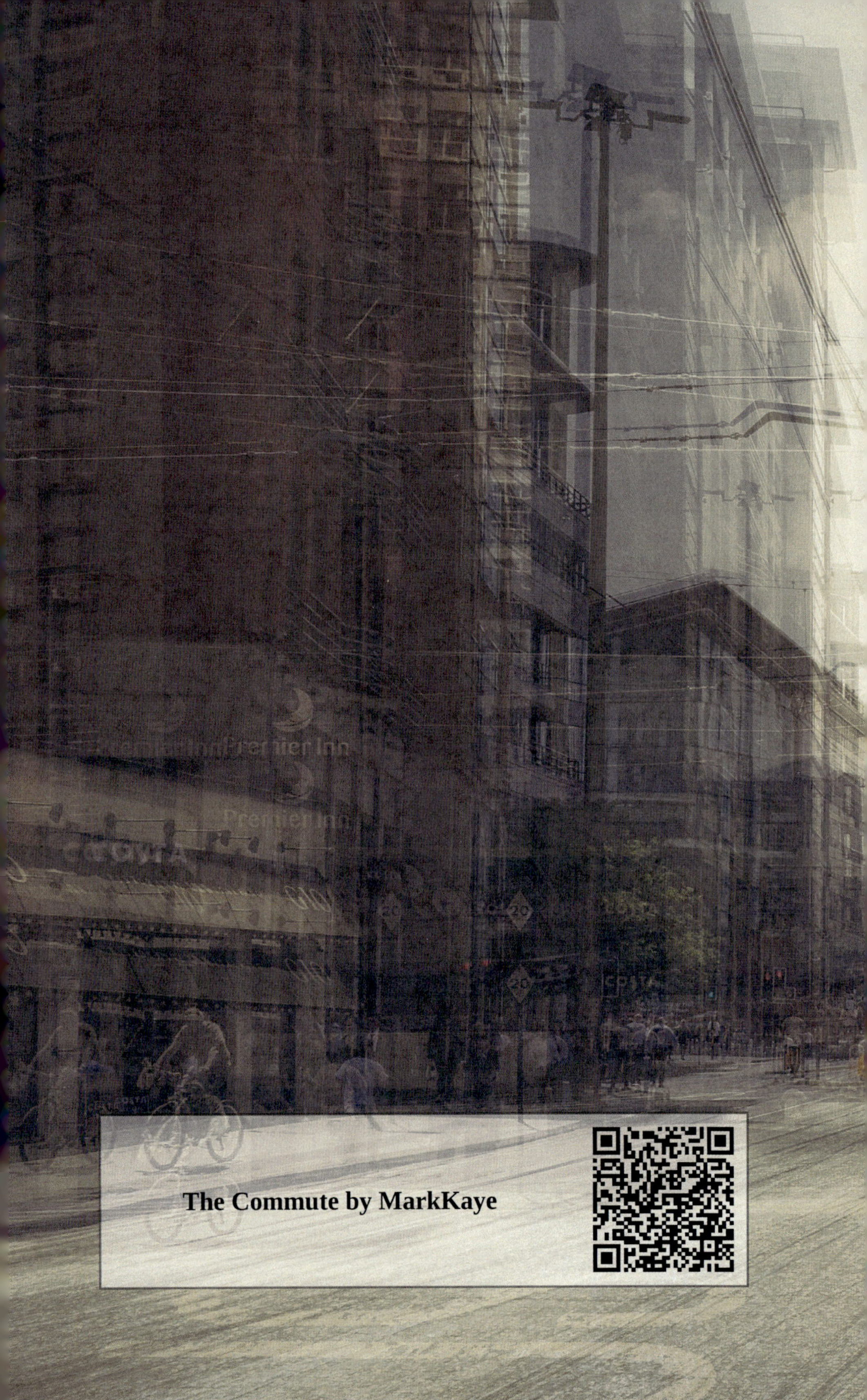

The Commute by MarkKaye

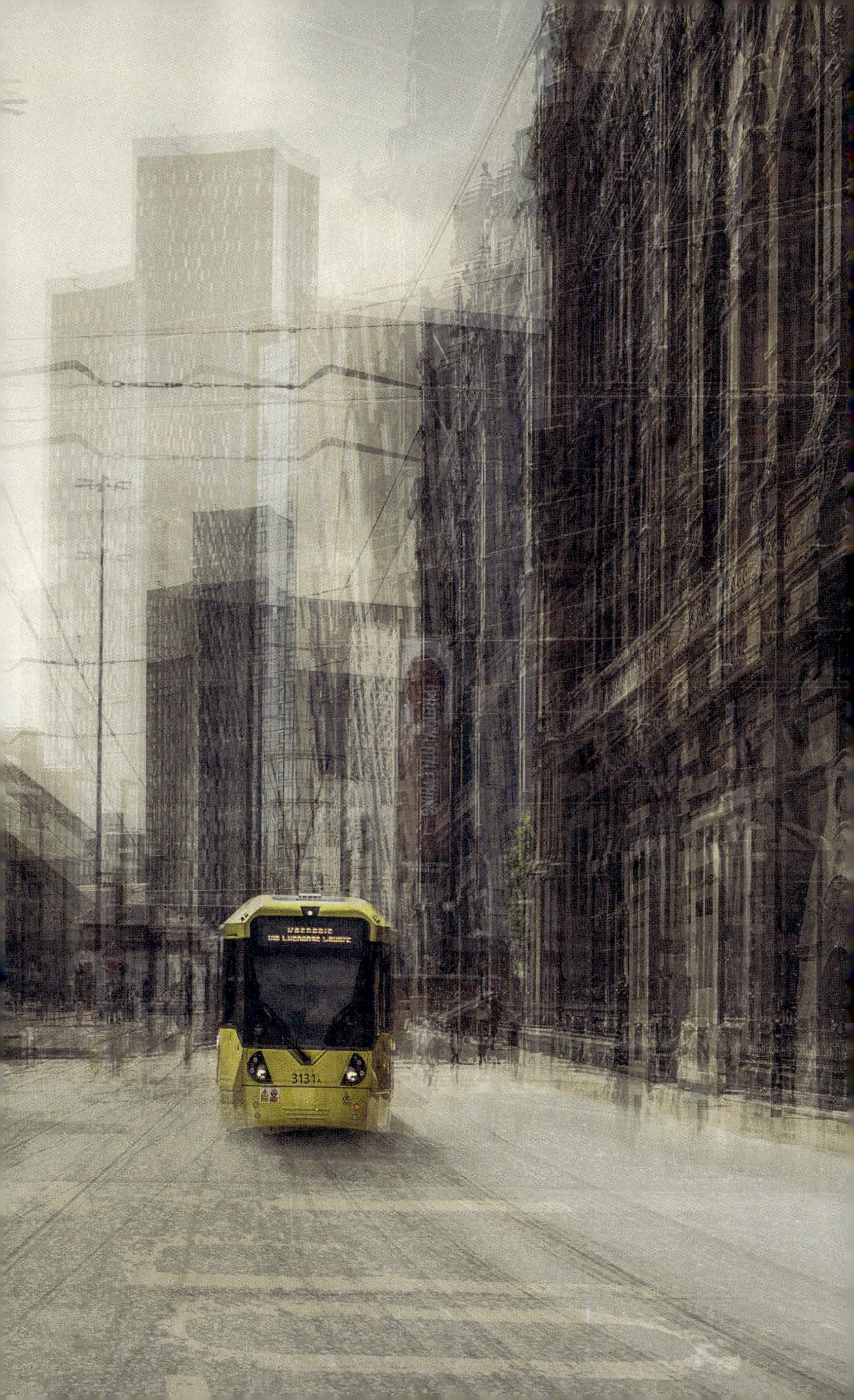
3131A

are still influenced by traditional power structures and wealth accumulation. As a result, people tend to gravitate toward influential figures and platforms driven by monetary gain, further contributing to centralization within the ecosystem.

True decentralization requires active participation and responsibility from all participants. It necessitates a level of knowledge and understanding that empowers individuals to make informed decisions and contribute meaningfully to the ecosystem. However, in practice, achieving such a comprehensive level of decentralization is incredibly challenging, given the diversity of knowledge, motivations, and capabilities within the community.

In the pursuit of a truly decentralized ecosystem, the question of anonymity and transparency becomes paramount. While decentralization aims to distribute decision-making power and ownership across a community, it does not necessarily imply that the key players driving the economy should remain anonymous.

Maintaining anonymity among decision-makers raises concerns about trust and accountability. In a decentralized system, participants need to have confidence in those guiding the direction of the community and the economy. Relying solely on profile pictures or words shared on social platforms may not be sufficient to instill trust. Participants seek concrete evidence of competence, responsibility, and genuine care for the collective well-being.

To uphold the principles of a decentralized system, participants must be able to identify and hold accountable those who are influencing the ecosystem. Transparency and clear lines of communication are vital for building trust and fostering collaboration. By knowing who the decision-makers are, participants can have more meaningful interactions, share insights, and collectively shape the community's future.

Anonymity, while it may provide privacy for individual participants, can also create a barrier to fostering a sense of responsibility and shared commitment. It is also one of the key barriers hindering the mass adoption of this truly remarkable technology. In a true decentralized system, the ability to take care of each other and ourselves is of paramount importance. Trusting an anonymous player to make significant decisions for the community can be challenging, as it lacks the transparency needed for collective confidence and cohesion.

Influencers, Thought Leaders, and Regulations

Influencers sometimes cause more problems and harm than help due to various reasons. Many influencers gain popularity based on their social media presence, but they may lack deep expertise or knowledge in the areas they promote. Consequently, their advice or recommendations may be misleading or inaccurate, leading to potential harm.

Moreover, some influencers unintentionally or deliberately spread misinformation, conspiracy theories, or false claims, especially if they have a large following. This can contribute to the dissemination of harmful beliefs and unfounded rumors, impacting their followers negatively.

Additionally, influencers often present an idealized version of their lives, creating unrealistic expectations and fostering feelings of inadequacy among their followers. This can lead to mental health issues and have a negative impact on self-esteem.

Furthermore, in their pursuit of sponsorships and collaborations, influencers may endorse products or practices that can be harmful to their followers. This can include promoting dangerous diets, untested supplements, or questionable beauty products.

The lack of accountability in the influencer industry can exacerbate the potential for harm, as some influencers prioritize personal gains over the well-being of their audience, ignoring the consequences of their actions or statements.

Moreover, influencers' promotion of a materialistic lifestyle centered around possessions can contribute to increased consumerism and excessive spending among their followers, leading to environmental issues and financial strain.

Lastly, some influencers may perpetuate cyberbullying or engage in toxic behavior online, either directly or indirectly, through their followers. This can cause significant harm to individuals' mental health and well-being.

To mitigate the potential harm caused by influencers, both influencers, and their followers should be critical consumers of content, fact-check information, and consider the consequences of the messages being shared. Encouraging the responsible use of social media and promoting positive values can help create a more constructive digital environment.

The difference between influencers and thought leaders lies in their approach, expertise, and impact on their respective audiences. Influencers typically have a large following on social media platforms and other digital channels, focusing on building their personal brand, lifestyle, and image. Their content often revolves around product endorsements, sponsored posts, and promoting brands, aiming to drive engagement and monetize their online presence.

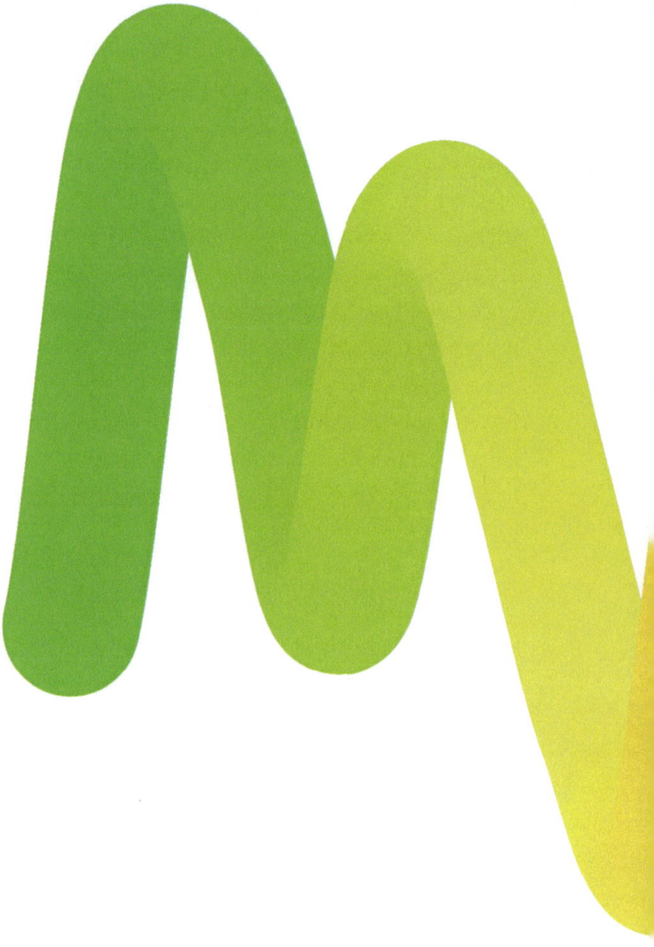

Chromie Squiggle #1194 by Snowfro

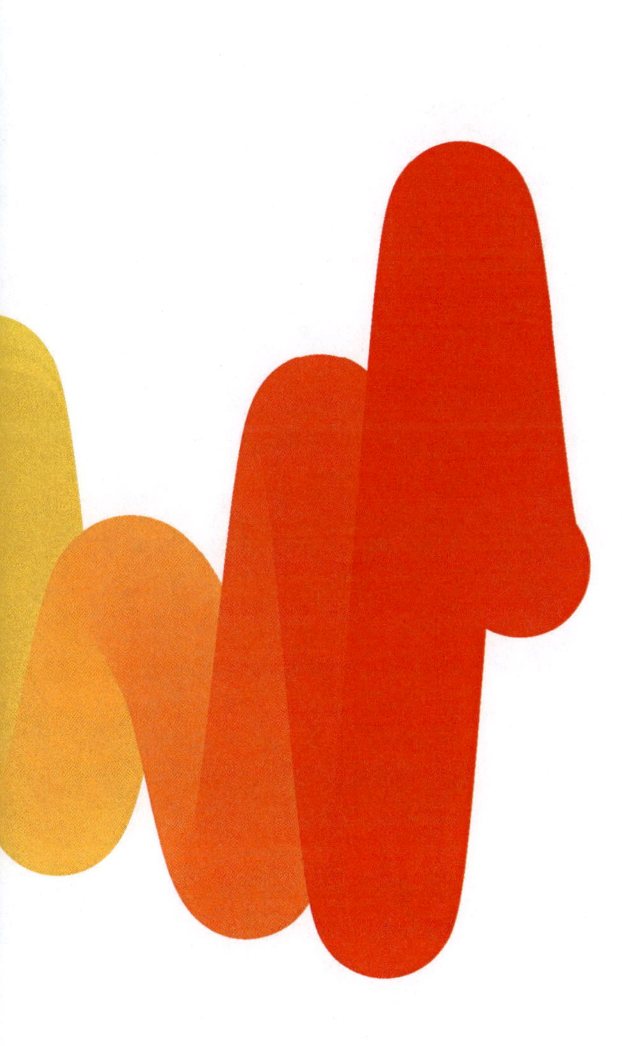

In contrast, thought leaders are individuals who are recognized as experts or authorities in a particular field or subject matter. They establish themselves as knowledgeable and credible sources through their expertise, experience, and contributions to their industry. Thought leaders focus on sharing insights, ideas, and innovative solutions to complex problems, inspiring and influencing others through their expertise and thought-provoking content.

While influencers may not necessarily possess in-depth expertise in the topics they promote, their popularity is based on their ability to connect with their audience, create engaging content, and leverage social media algorithms for visibility. On the other hand, thought leaders are known for their deep knowledge and authority in their chosen area of specialization, often gained through years of honing their skills and contributing to their field through research, publications, or practical applications.

In terms of impact and influence, influencers excel in promoting products and services, having a significant impact on consumer behavior and brand perception. Their endorsements can lead to increased sales and brand awareness, but their influence is often more short-term and transactional.

Conversely, thought leaders have a long-lasting and profound influence on their audiences. They can shape industry trends, drive innovation, and inspire others to take action based on their ideas and insights. Their influence extends beyond product promotions, focusing on broader issues and challenging conventional thinking.

The dominance of influencers in the NFT space has resulted in a significant number of pump-and-dump schemes, where certain NFT projects are artificially hyped and then quickly abandoned, causing financial losses for unsuspecting investors. This behavior is driven by the general public's preference for following influencers rather than seeking guidance from thought leaders with genuine expertise in the field.

The consequences of this behavior are detrimental to the NFT ecosystem. Pump-and-dump schemes not only lead to financial losses for investors but also erode trust in the overall legitimacy and credibility of the NFT market. It creates a volatile and speculative environment that detracts from the true potential of NFTs as a valuable and transformative technology for artists and collectors alike.

To address this issue, it is crucial to educate the general public about the risks associated with following influencers blindly and participating in pump-and-dump schemes. Increased awareness about the importance of seeking advice from thought leaders who possess genuine expertise and a long-term vision for the NFT space can help individuals make more informed decisions.

Platforms and marketplaces can play a significant role in promoting transparency and responsible behavior. Implementing stricter guidelines to identify and prevent pump-and-dump schemes, as well as promoting the works of credible artists and projects through verification and validation processes, can foster a more trustworthy NFT ecosystem.

Encouraging more meaningful engagement and discussions around NFT projects that focus on artistic value, innovation, and long-term potential can also shift the public's attention from short-term gains to the genuine value and impact of NFT art and technology.

Ultimately, fostering a community that values thought leadership, ethical practices, and genuine artistic contributions can help create a more sustainable and authentic NFT space that benefits artists, collectors, and investors alike.

The role of governments and regulatory bodies in the NFT space is multifaceted, as they aim to strike a balance between promoting accountability, protecting the general public, and fostering the future growth of the technology while respecting its decentralized nature.

Governments can establish regulatory frameworks that outline clear guidelines for influencers and NFT projects to adhere to. These frameworks can include measures to prevent fraudulent practices, promote transparency in disclosures, and protect consumers from scams and misleading information.

Regulatory bodies can play a critical role in safeguarding the interests of the general public by monitoring and investigating instances of fraud, misinformation, and pump-and-dump schemes. They can take action against individuals or entities that engage in deceptive practices to ensure fair treatment for investors and consumers.

Authorities can work with industry experts and thought leaders to establish processes for verifying and validating NFT projects and influencers. This can help distinguish legitimate projects from potential scams, providing a higher level of confidence for investors and collectors.

Governments should promote educational initiatives to inform the public about the risks and benefits of participating in the NFT space. By raising awareness about responsible practices and the potential consequences of engaging with certain influencers or projects, individuals can make more informed decisions.

Authorities can collaborate with industry stakeholders, including artists, platforms, and marketplaces, to develop best practices and self-regulatory mechanisms. This approach allows for industry expertise to influence regulatory decisions while respecting the decentralized nature of blockchain technology.

While ensuring accountability, authorities can also foster a supportive environment for innovation in the NFT space. This includes recognizing the transformative potential of NFTs in art and technology and encouraging responsible experimentation and creative expression.

While enforcing accountability, it is essential for governments to acknowledge and embrace the decentralized nature of NFT technology. Striking a balance between regulation and maintaining the open and permissionless nature of blockchain technology can support the growth of the NFT space while preserving its core principles.

By adopting a balanced approach that encourages innovation and creativity while holding influencers and projects accountable for their actions, governments and regulatory bodies can contribute to the long-term sustainability and growth of the NFT space, protecting the interests of the general public and fostering a vibrant and responsible ecosystem.

Anonymity remains a significant concern in the current NFT space, posing a considerable challenge to achieving mass adoption. A substantial portion of participants, including project creators, artists, and collectors, prefer to remain anonymous for various reasons, further complicating matters.

During a workshop conducted by the UK-based auction house Bonhams in 2021, I emphasized the importance of addressing this issue. Consider a scenario where an individual purchases an NFT from an anonymous project. They may be drawn to the art, the community, or the potential for profit. However, the very next day, they find themselves confronted by the FBI or another authority, as they are suspected of having ties to a terrorist organization. Unbeknownst to them, the NFT collection they acquired was, in fact, a scheme orchestrated by a criminal group to fund their nefarious activities.

This example highlights the grave consequences of anonymity in the NFT space, consequences that not only affect current participants but also act as a substantial deterrent for newcomers. The fear of unknowingly engaging in illicit activities discourages potential users from fully embracing NFTs and the blockchain technology behind them.

Addressing anonymity-related concerns is crucial for the long-term success and mass adoption of NFTs. Striking a balance between privacy and accountability is essential for fostering a safe and trustworthy environment that encourages broader participation and ensures the integrity of the NFT ecosystem.

Finding a solution to the issue of anonymity in the NFT space is a crucial task that requires careful consideration and action. Two potential avenues for addressing this challenge are self-regulation by the community and intervention by authorities and regulators.

However, the likelihood of achieving self-regulation within the NFT community seems slim. Many participants, including influential figures, prefer to remain anonymous. As a result, establishing a collective system of accountability and transparency becomes challenging.

On the other hand, relying solely on regulatory intervention could prove detrimental to the NFT space. Harsh regulations imposed by authorities might stifle creativity, innovation, and the free flow of ideas within the decentralized ecosystem. They may also lead to a loss of the very essence that makes NFTs attractive in the first place–the ability to create and exchange assets without centralized control.

Striking a balance between self-regulation and external oversight is vital. A well-implemented and transparent self-regulation system within the NFT community could help build trust, foster accountability, and protect participants from malicious activities. However, to achieve widespread adoption and maintain the integrity of the NFT space, cooperation with regulators may also be necessary.

Collaboration with authorities can provide a framework for ensuring the safety and well-being of users while preserving the decentralized nature of NFT technology. By engaging in constructive dialogues with regulators, the NFT community can work toward finding practical solutions that allow for responsible growth, innovation, and inclusivity in this rapidly evolving landscape.

The Future of NFTs and Digital Art

Initially, when NFTs emerged in the art world, many artists were thrilled by the potential disappearance of so-called gatekeepers. Traditional art galleries had long held the reins when it came to marketing artist and their works, establishing an artist's career, strategizing their success, and connecting with collectors. However, these galleries also acted as gatekeepers, creating significant barriers for emerging artists to gain entry, and for those already represented, they would often levy exorbitant commissions, ranging from 50 to 70 percent, on each sale they facilitated. This frustrated artists, leading to their excitement about the possibilities offered by NFTs.

As time passed, some artists began to realize that they lacked the expertise to mark and brand their works, as well as set appropriate prices. They understood that to expand their reach and attract more collectors, they needed the support of galleries. However, this required a shift in galleries' practices, with greater fairness and consideration for artists' needs. The NFT space presented an opportunity for artists to explore new ways of collaboration and partnership with galleries, aiming for a more mutually beneficial relationship that fosters artistic growth and success.

One of the key observations that has shaped my perspective is the transformative power of social interaction within the NFT space. Through NFTs, I have not only connected with renowned artists but also formed deep and meaningful friendships with them. Interactions with people like Ryan (ThankYouX) and Keith Grossman highlight the profound sense of community and connection that NFTs foster.

Furthermore, the democratization of art in the digital realm has expanded the definition of what can be considered art. NFTs are challenging us to reconsider and expand our definition of art. Digital art, which was once seen as a fringe category, has now been thrust into the limelight, demanding recognition and respect. In this new era, creators using digital mediums such as animation, graphic design, and motion graphics are being rightfully acknowledged as artists. Their works, which were previously underappreciated or misunderstood, are now celebrated and sold as valuable art pieces.

This disruption of the traditional art scene has sparked debates and controversies, but it has also opened doors for countless artists to express themselves and be recognized for their unique contributions. Critics argue that the sudden surge in NFT art production is driven more by profit-seeking motives by artistic integrity. While there may be some truth to this viewpoint, it is crucial to remember that art has always evolved alongside technology. Throughout history, new artistic mediums have often been met with skepticism and resistance. The introduction of photography, for example, was initially considered a threat to traditional painting. Yet, over time, it carved out its own unique place in the art world and is now universally recognized as a legitimate and respected art form. Similarly, NFTs and digital art are

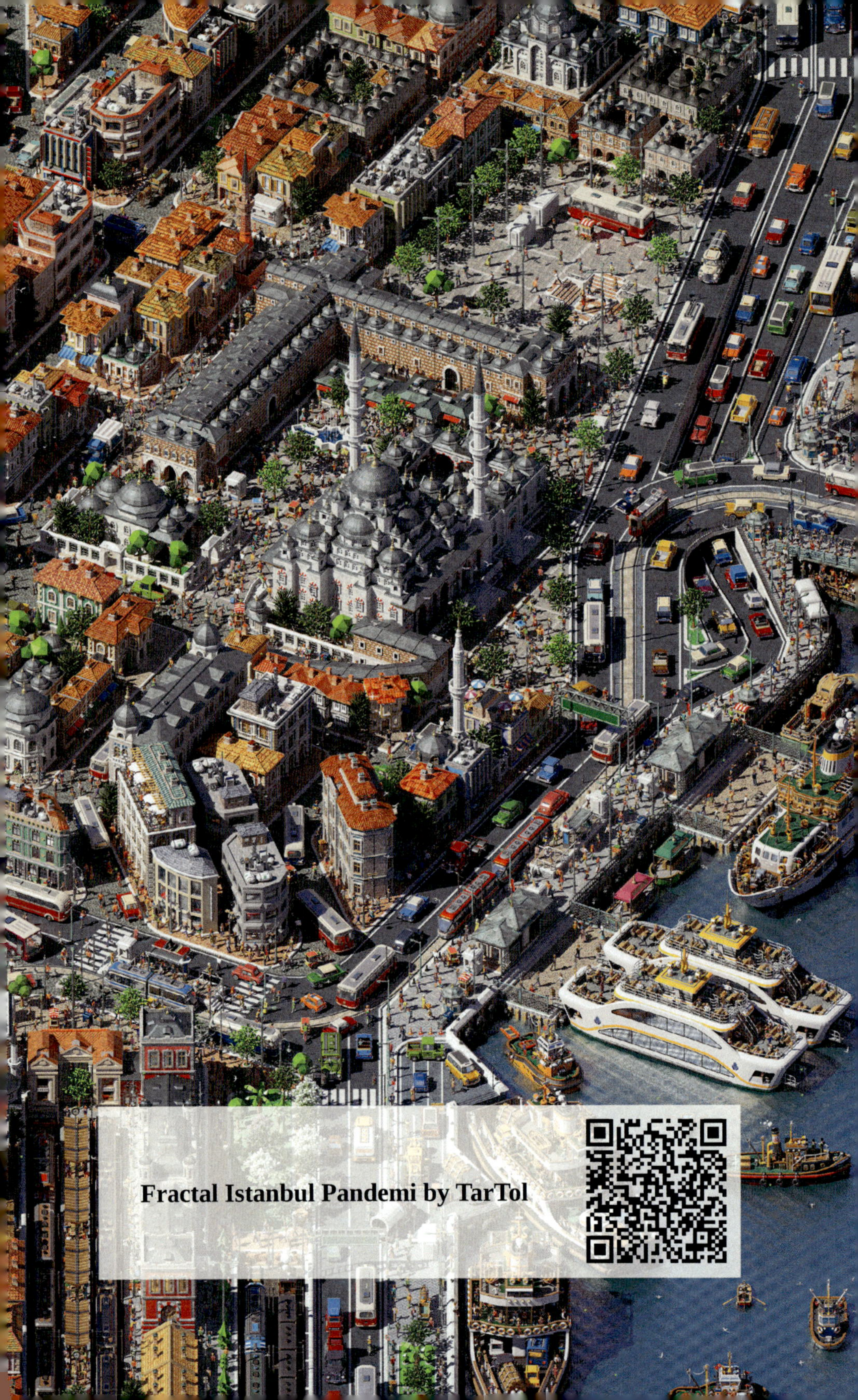

Fractal Istanbul Pandemi by TarTol

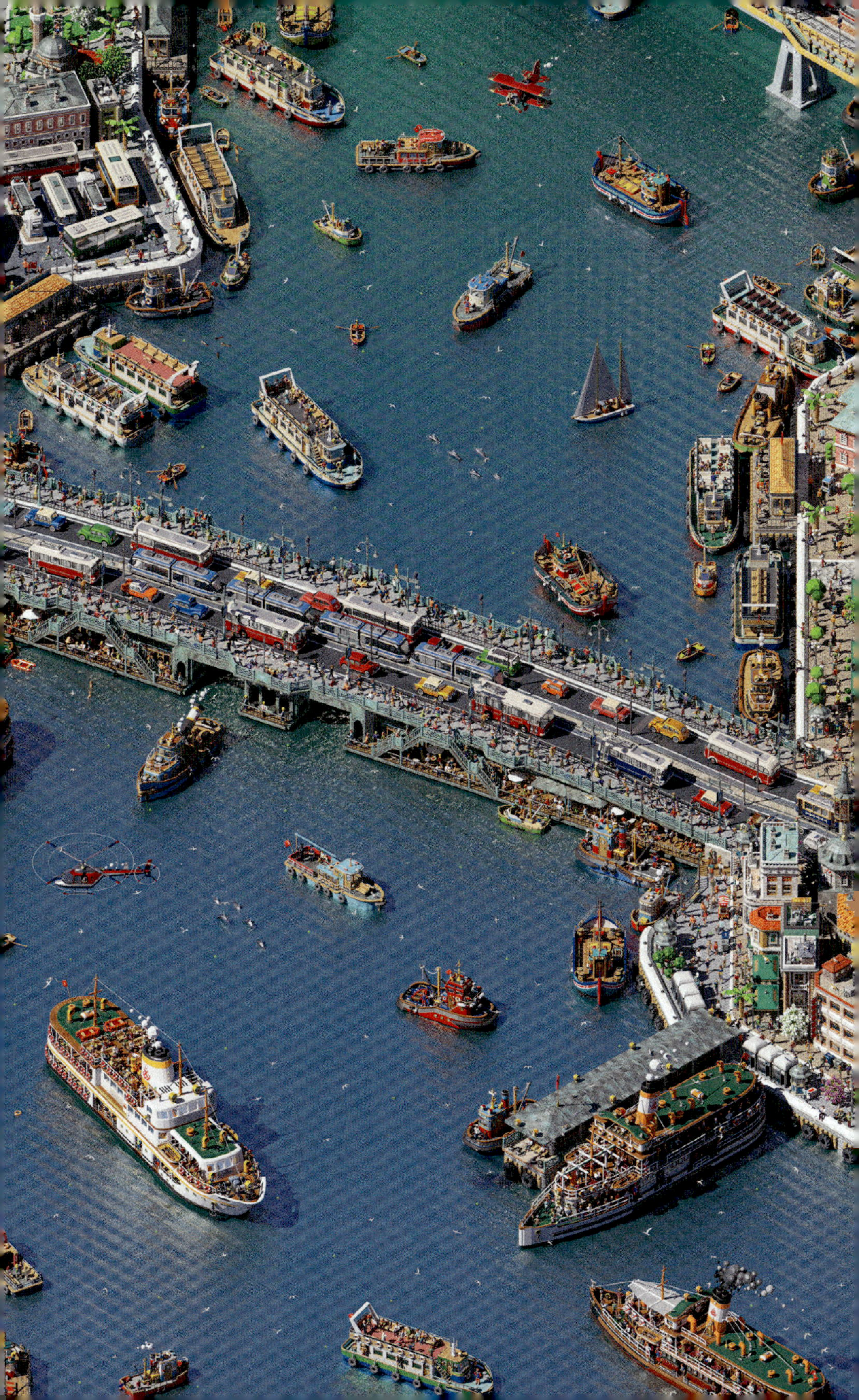

disrupting the conventional art scene, challenging our preconceived notions and forcing us to question and redefine what art can be. They are not mere digital renditions of physical paintings or sculptures; they represent new forms of expression that are inherently tied to the digital space.

Another example of the challenges associated with the acceptance of a new digital version of the same technology is the transition from physical newspapers to digital news platforms. With the advent of the internet and digital technology, traditional print newspapers faced significant disruptions to their business model. Many people had been accustomed to reading physical newspapers for generations, and the shift to digital news platforms presented challenges in terms of acceptance and adaptation.

Initially, some readers were resistant to the idea of consuming news digitally, as they were used to the tangible experience of holding a physical newspaper and flipping through its pages. There were concerns about the reliability of digital news sources, the user experience of reading news on screens, and the potential loss of jobs in the print newspaper industry.

However, as digital technology improved, online news platforms became more user-friendly, and as people increasingly adopted smartphones and tablets, the acceptance of digital news grew. Over time, many newspapers had to adapt and develop their online presence to remain relevant and reach a broader audience.

The shift from physical newspapers to digital news platforms also addressed the issue of distance and accessibility. Before the digital era, reading a newspaper from a different country or region required physical delivery, which could take several days or even weeks. People living outside the circulation area of a specific newspaper often had limited access to timely news from other regions.

With the advent of digital news platforms, this geographical barrier was overcome. Anyone with internet access could now read news from anywhere in the world instantly. Digital newspapers allowed people , regardless of their location, to access news content in real-time, making information more readily available and breaking down the barriers of distance.

This increased accessibility not only benefited readers but also created new opportunities for newspapers to expand their reach and readership globally. Newspapers that previously had a limited local audience could now attract readers from different parts of the world, leading to a broader and more diverse readership base.

The true value of art, whether it is a traditional painting or an NFT, lies not solely in the medium itself, but also in its ability to evoke emotions, communicate ideas, and reflect the society in which it was created. The medium serves as a vessel, a means of conveying the artist's message to the viewer. The artistic essence and impact of a piece extend far beyond the medium it employs.

Ultimately, it is crucial to appreciate and evaluate artworks based on their artistic merit, their ability to resonate with audiences, and their capacity to spark meaningful conversations. By embracing the transformative potential of digital art, we can break free from traditional constraints and explore new frontiers of creativity, allowing the medium to inspire and challenge our understanding of art itself.

As the NFT space continues to evolve, it is important to consider the role of blockchain technology. While blockchain currently underpins the NFT ecosystem, I envision a future where its presence becomes more seamless and transparent, fading into the background as the focus shifts to the art itself and the narratives it represents. Blockchain's immutability and trustless nature will continue to provide invaluable benefits in terms of provenance and ownership verification, and the technical intricacies will become less prominent.

In terms of financial transactions, cryptocurrency has played a significant role in the early adoption of NFTs. However, as the market matures, I anticipate a diversification of payment methods, with cryptocurrencies becoming just one of many options available to collectors. This shift will make NFTs more accessible and inclusive to a broader audience, fostering greater adoption and participation.

While there are promising prospects on the horizon, challenges also loom. The democratization of art means that more creators are entering the space, leading to increased competition and discoverability issues. However, innovation and technology will pave the way for solutions. My team and I at Mondoir are actively working on tools to help artists navigate this expanding universe, ensuring their works receive the attention they deserve.

It is essential to remain grounded and acknowledge that the NFT space will face its share of roadblocks and hurdles. However, with a spirit of resilience and a commitment to fostering meaningful connections and empowering artists, we can collectively shape a future where NFTs and digital art thrive, making a lasting impact on the art world as we know it.

I envision a future where digital art takes center stage, much like the transformation we witnessed in the realm of photography. Just as the introduction of digital cameras initially faced resistance from traditional photographers, the acceptance of digital art and NFTs may encounter similar skepticism. However, as digital cameras and digital photos have integrated into our daily lives alongside traditional photography, digital art will dominate while traditional art forms will continue to hold their own significance and value.

In today's world, we witness a similar phenomenon with handmade versus machine-made products. While machine-made goods have become widely prevalent, there remains a dedicated market and audience for handmade items, which often command higher prices. This parallel can be drawn to the future of art. Digital art will undoubtedly become the dominant form, offering exciting possibilities and widespread accessibility. However, traditional art forms will persist, cherished for their unique qualities and the human touch they embody.

Furthermore, the rise of AI and its potential to generate content and artwork should not diminish the importance of works created through human effort and expression. While AI-driven creations may streamline content production across various sectors, there will always be a distinct value attributed to handmade and artist-driven works. These pieces, rooted in the passion, vision, and personal touch of the artist, will continue to hold a special place and resonate with audiences seeking the authenticity and soulful connection that only human creativity can provide.

I hold a strong belief that AI, much like any other technology, can serve as a valuable tool for creators. While machines can produce or replicate artworks, the essence of creative brilliance often originates from the mind of a human artist. As we embrace the future, AI will undoubtedly play a significant role, especially in the realm of digital art. Even though a machine may generate an image, the initial design or the final touch is a result of human creativity.

In the world of digital art driven by AI, there is a fascinating interplay between humans and machines. Just as a beautifully written poem can evoke powerful emotions in the reader's mind, the very prompt that leads to the creation of an AI-generated image can be considered art in itself. The creative spark that inspires the AI's output holds a profound artistic value. It reflects the ingenuity and imagination of the human artist who set the parameters and guided the AI's creative journey.

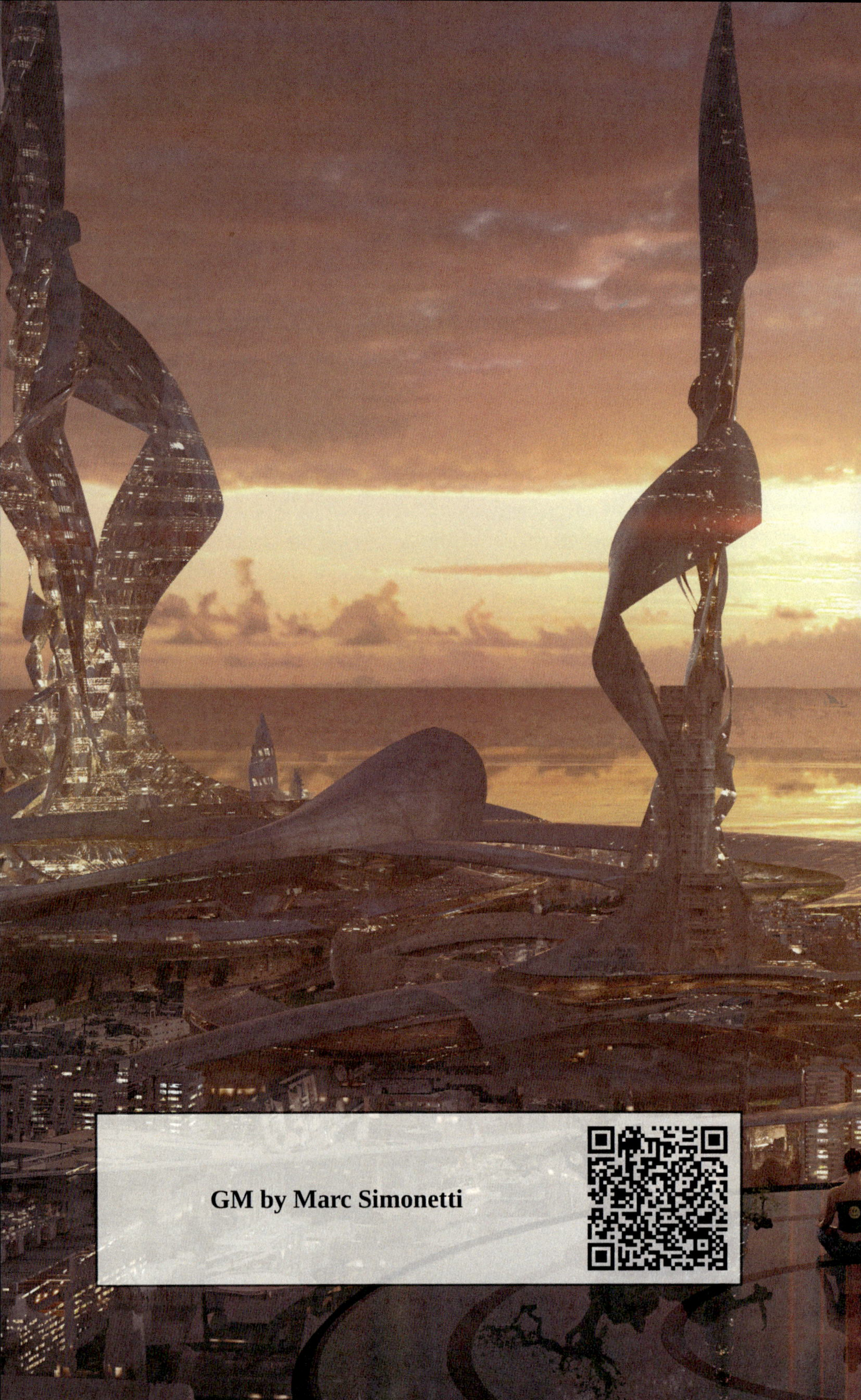
GM by Marc Simonetti

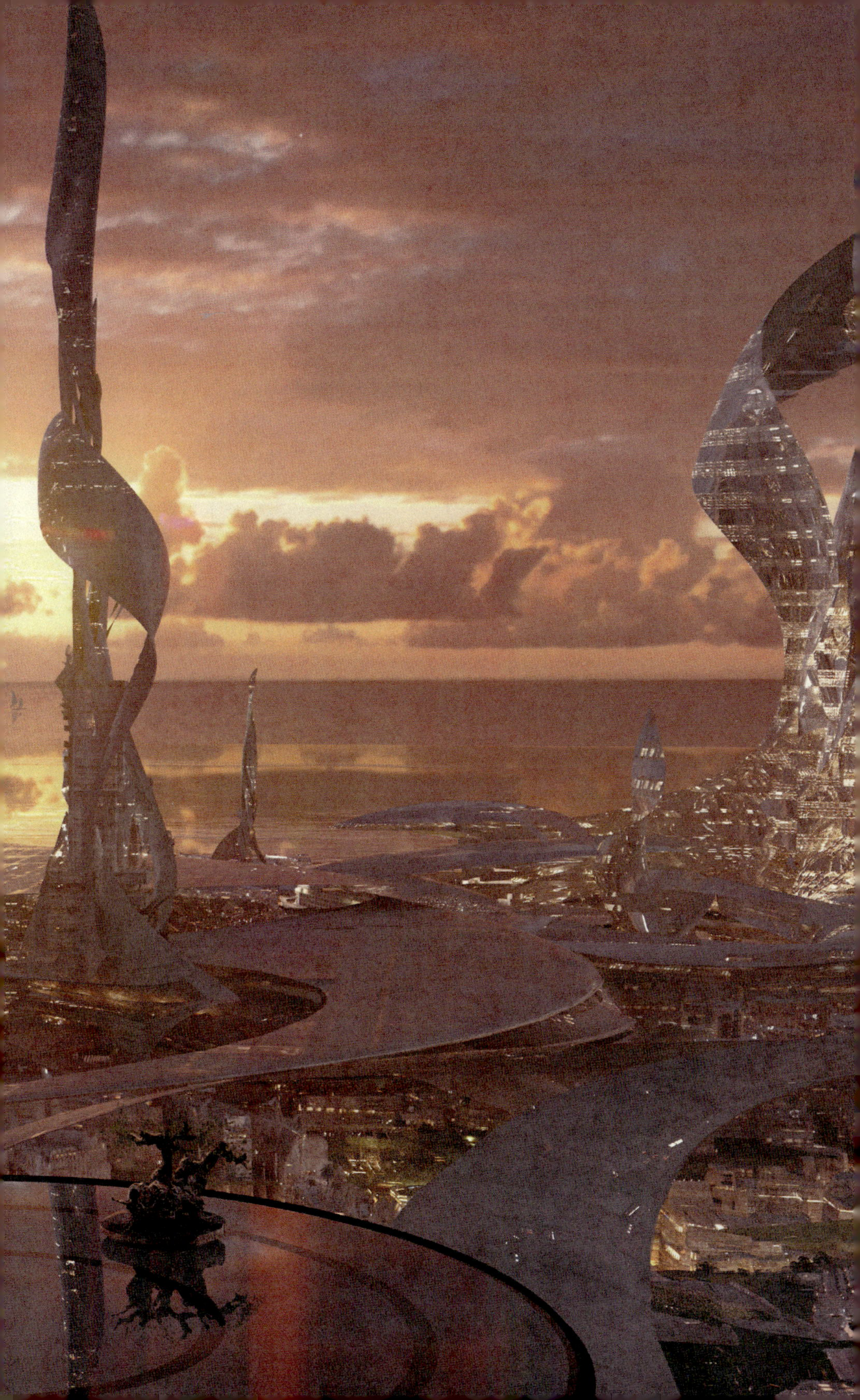

Ultimately, AI is not a replacement for the artist's vision but rather an extension of their capabilities. The collaboration between human creativity and AI technology opens up new avenues for artistic expression, challenging traditional boundaries and redefining what art can be in the digital age. By embracing AI as a creative aid, artists can explore uncharted territories and unlock new dimensions of their own artistic journey.

Envisioning the vast potential of NFTs as the underlying technology capable of representing any digital asset, I see a future where their applications extend far beyond the realm of art. It is not just about digital art; it's about transforming the way we interact with essential aspects of our lives.

In this future, the concept of NFTs extends to our very identities, where documents like driving licenses and passports are seamlessly tokenized as NFTs. Blockchain technology would power this transformation, offering consumers a simplified, user-friendly experience without the need to grapple with its complexities. This shift would revolutionize the way we manage our personal information, ensuring its security and immutability.

Beyond identity documents, the potential of NFTs extends to revolutionizing record-keeping in various domains. Medical records, educational transcripts, historical archives, and ownership papers would all be transitioned to this more sustainable, environmentally friendly method of storage and trust. The reliance on paper documents, which contributes to deforestation, would be replaced, and our records would find a secure home on the blockchain.

Moreover, NFTs would revolutionize the ticketing industry. Tickets for various events, whether for travel, sports, or concerts, would be moved to blockchains. With NFTs, the concept of proven ownership, provenance, and tamper-proof records would eliminate the possibility of forged tickets being sold on the black market. Sporting organizations like FIFA would have a more robust and transparent system to control ticket sales and ensure artists, teams, and organizers receive their deserved royalties.

The future would also bring about a paradigm shift in property transactions. Buying and selling properties online would become a trivial process with the aid of NFTs. Ownership of a property could be securely represented on your phone or a secure device, streamlining the way we interact with real estate.

In this vision, NFTs usher in an era of innovation, efficiency, and environmental consciousness. The possibilities seem limitless, and as we embrace this transformative technology, we are poised to experience a future that is truly amazing with NFTs.

My Role in the Future of Digital Art and NFTs

NFTs and digital art continue to evolve, and I intend to participate actively, leveraging my experience and resources to contribute to their growth and maturation.

For one, I plan on continuing my efforts to support lesser-known artists. I strongly believe in the democratization of the art world and that talented artists from all corners of the world should have their shot at recognition and success. As a part of this, I will continue to acquire works from emerging artists, not only enriching my own collection but also helping these artists gain exposure.

Additionally, I recognize the struggle that artists face in standing out amid the increasing saturation of the digital art world. To that end, I am committed to developing tools and platforms that aid in the discovery of artists and their works. These tools will not only connect artists with potential collectors but also provide a structure to the otherwise chaotic world of digital art.

Furthermore, I plan to push for more transparency in the space. Blockchain technology has already proven its potential for providing a trustworthy record of provenance, but there's still much more we can do. For example, clear guidelines on intellectual property rights and royalties, as well as strict consequences for those who infringe on them, are necessary steps toward a healthier ecosystem.

As an individual collector and an NFT enthusiast, I understand the transformative power of NFTs in reshaping the traditional art world. However, this is not a journey I can undertake alone. It requires the collective effort of artists, collectors, developers, and enthusiasts from all walks of life. Therefore, I am dedicated to fostering a community that is open to dialogue, collaboration, and mutual growth.

Lastly, I aspire to continue my journey as a creator. The experience of minting my own NFTs, whether to raise funds for a cause or just to express my creativity, has been deeply fulfilling. I look forward to creating more unique pieces and perhaps inspiring others to do the same.

While I may not possess the skills of a traditional artist, I, like any individual, am filled with dreams, emotions, and vivid scenes that I long to express and share with the world. The desire to translate these inner visions into tangible creations is an innate human instinct. Though I may lack expertise in using a brush or wielding a pencil, the emergence of blockchain technology and NFTs has opened up a whole new world of creative possibilities for someone like me.

In this new era, the barriers to artistic expression have been broken down. The conventional norms that once dictated who could be an artist and what constituted "art" have been challenged. Now, anyone with a vision and passion can create and record their imagination on the blockchain. With the aid of NFTs, these digital creations can be securely preserved and presented to the world.

For me, the allure of this technological revolution lies in the freedom it offers. I am no longer constrained by traditional mediums or the need for artistic mastery. The NFT space has become a canvas where my thoughts, emotions, and ideas can flourish, regardless of whether I can paint or draw.

With every creation I mint as an NFT, I am offering a glimpse into my mind and soul, allowing others to witness my inner world. The interpretation and impact of my art now lie in the hands of the viewers, adding an exciting layer of interaction and engagement to the artistic process.

In this boundless digital realm, the distinction between the creator and the spectator blurs, fostering an environment of inclusivity and creativity. Each NFT becomes a unique and authentic representation of an individual's thoughts and dreams, an authentic piece of their essence, shared with a global audience.

This newfound power to express, record, and share my visions through NFTs has been a revelation. My lack of traditional artistic skills no longer limits me; instead, I embrace the boundless possibilities that this technology offers. As an artist in this new era, my creations find their place in a world where creativity knows no bounds and everyone's voice can be heard and appreciated.

As I close this narrative, I am filled with gratitude for my experiences and the remarkable individuals I have encountered on this journey. From the inspiring creators pushing the boundaries of their craft to the enthusiastic collectors celebrating and supporting these artists, the world of NFTs and digital art has proven to be an extraordinary microcosm of innovation, passion, and mutual support.

Conclusion

My journey into the realm of NFTs and digital art was born out of curiosity, driven by the thrill of discovery, and cemented by the transformative power of technology to connect and enable creators worldwide.

I started as an observer, became a participant, and gradually evolved into a catalyst, working to empower artists and solve real-world problems through the magic of NFTs. From contributing to charities and launching innovative projects to opening a gallery space and leading the charge to democratize art, the journey has been a rewarding and eye-opening experience.

The leaps and bounds made by NFTs and blockchain technology are a testament to human creativity and resilience. But as we march forward, we must keep sight of the foundational principles that make this space so special: decentralization, inclusivity, and respect for creators.

I have shared my journey not as a blueprint for success but as a mosaic of experiences that demonstrate the diverse paths that exist in this space. Each individual's journey will be unique, filled with their own successes, failures, discoveries, and lessons. My story serves as a catalyst, sparking curiosity and inspiring you to explore the limitless possibilities that lie in the realm of NFTs and digital art.

Throughout my journey in the NFT space, I have had the incredible privilege of forming deep connections and friendships with many talented artists and creators. It has been an honor to get to know them on a personal level, spend time with them, learn from their experiences, and gain insights into their creative processes.

My encounters with renowned personalities like Keith Grossman, Paris Hilton, and MC Hammer are a testament to the incredible convergence of diverse communities that the NFT space has enabled. From being an ordinary collector with no connection to celebrities, NFTs brought me into contact with well-known figures and allowed me to contribute to causes and projects that I believe in.

But it is not just about the high-profile figures. It is also about the artists and creatives who, for the first time, have found a global platform where they can truly shine, as well as the countless individuals and communities that have benefited from charity projects powered by NFTs. It is a testament to the transformative power of technology–an affirmation that when wielded with purpose, technology can be a tool for good.

Among the many remarkable individuals I have had the pleasure of connecting with are ThankYouX, DeeKay, Carlos Luna James, Parin Heidari, BT, Jake-Andrews, FEWOCiOUS, Raphaël Erba, and Christian Burns. These artists and creators have not only inspired me with their immense talent and creativity, but they have also become cherished friends within the NFT community.

Additionally, I have had the privilege of connecting with other influential figures in the NFT space–such as Mehdi Abbasian, who is not only my cofounder at Mondoir but also a dear friend. We have shared our journeys, exchanged ideas, and worked toward common goals within the NFT ecosystem.

Tom Brackey, a well-known and highly successful lawyer and tech entrepreneur, emerged as a key figure in my journey and Mondoir through our shared involvement in the NFT space. His unparalleled expertise, vast connections, and strategic guidance continue to shape our endeavors in this emerging landscape.

These friendships and connections have enriched my NFT experience in profound ways. They have provided me with unique perspectives, opportunities for collaboration, and a sense of camaraderie within the vibrant and ever-evolving NFT community. I am grateful for the bonds I have formed with these incredible individuals, and I look forward to the continued growth and exploration that lies ahead in this remarkable space.

As it stands, with the art and technology worlds at a crossroads, reflecting on my journey while anticipating an exciting future, my hope is that this story inspires you. Whether you are an artist looking to make your mark, a collector seeking unique treasures, a technologist exploring new frontiers, or simply someone curious about the world of NFTs and digital art, I hope this narrative provides a valuable perspective.

The future of NFTs is still being written, and can be a part of that narrative. Whether as a creator, collector, innovator, or simply a spectator, your participation contributes to the vibrancy and dynamism of this space.

So, I invite you to step into this world, immerse yourself in its wonders, learn, contribute, and make your mark. The world of NFTs is waiting to welcome you with open arms.

Frequently Asked Questions

What are NFTs?

NFTs, or Non-Fungible Tokens, are a type of cryptocurrency that represent ownership of unique digital assets. Unlike traditional cryptocurrencies such as Bitcoin, NFTs cannot be exchanged on a one-to-one basis as they each hold distinct values and characteristics.

How do NFTs work?

NFTs are created using blockchain technology, specifically on platforms like Ethereum. Each NFT is assigned a unique digital signature that verifies its authenticity and ownership. A blockchain provides an immutable and transparent record of the asset's history, including details about its creator and previous owners.

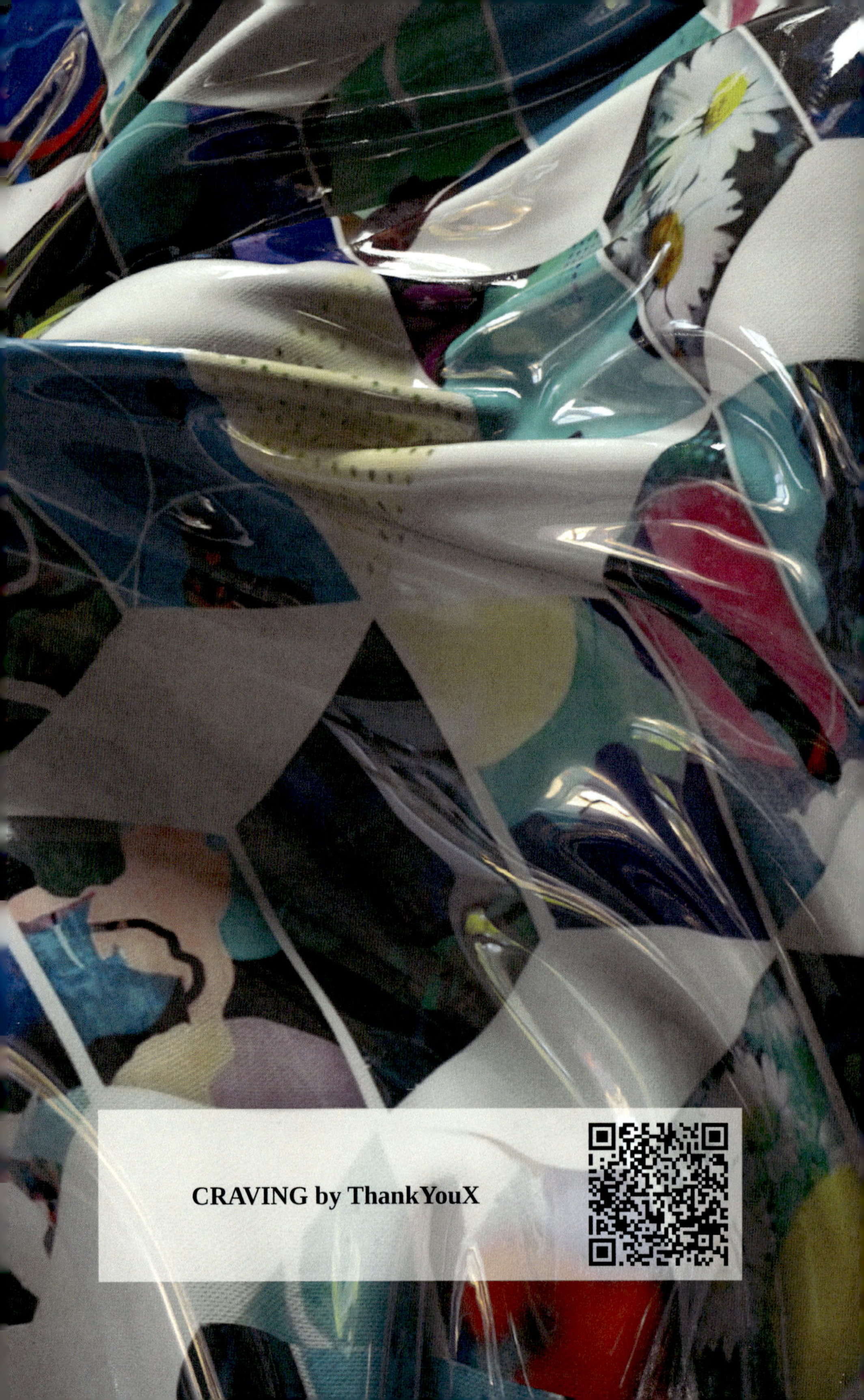
CRAVING by ThankYouX

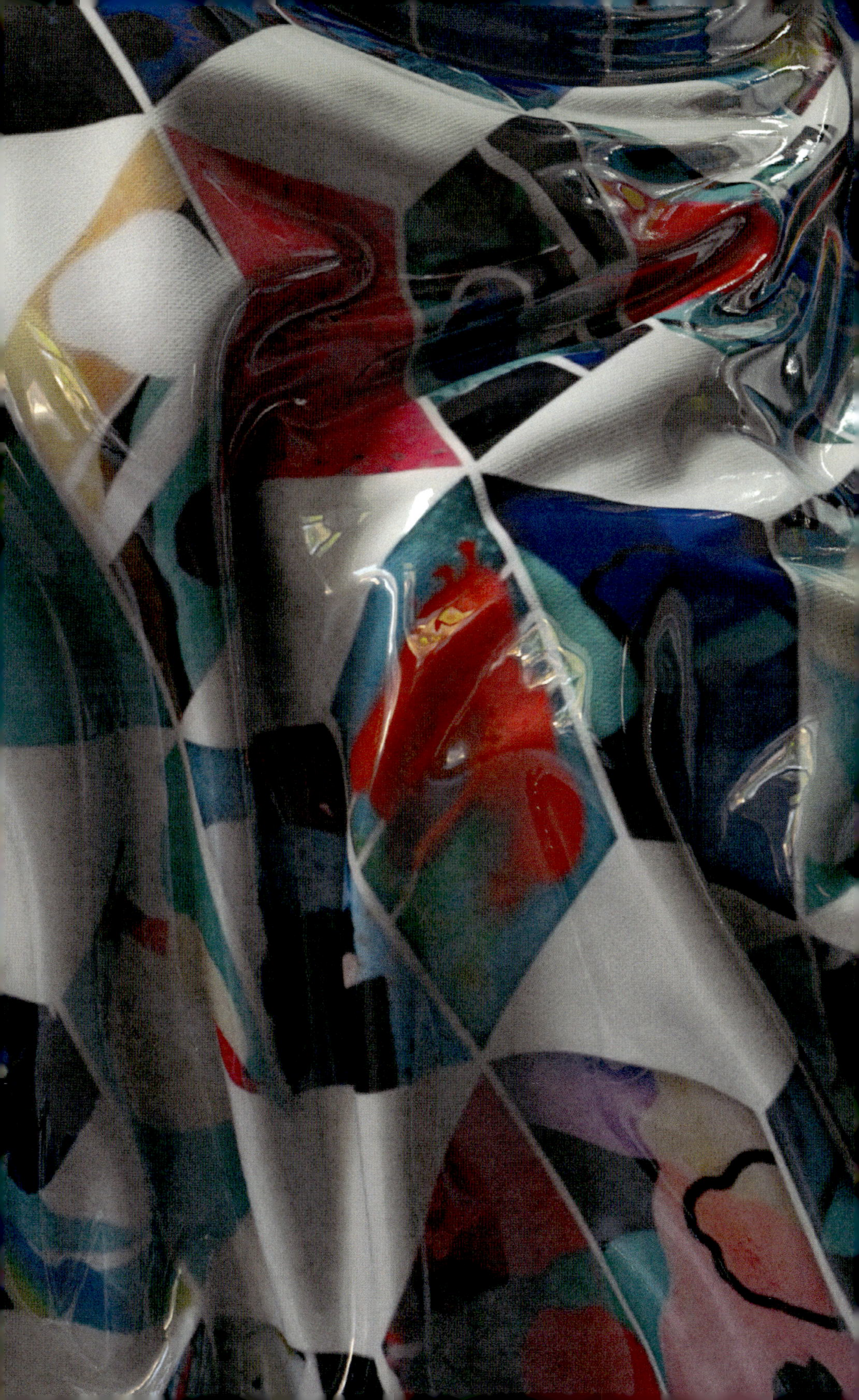

What kinds of digital assets can be represented as NFTs?

NFTs can represent a wide range of digital assets, including digital art, music, videos, virtual real estate, collectibles, and even tweets or articles. Essentially, any digital content that can be stored and tokenized can be turned into an NFT.

Are NFTs just a fad or a passing trend?

While the NFT space has seen explosive growth and media attention in recent years, it is more than just a passing trend. NFTs have introduced a paradigm shift in ownership and creativity, allowing for the direct support of artists and creation of unique digital art forms. As blockchain technology continues to evolve, NFTs are likely to play an increasingly important role in various sectors.

How do NFTs impact the art world?

NFTs have revolutionized the art world by providing artists with a direct and transparent means of monetizing their digital creations. They offer a secure and verifiable method of proving ownership and provenance, reducing issues of forgery and disputes. NFTs have also democratized the art market, allowing artists to bypass traditional gatekeepers and connect directly with their audiences.

What is the environmental impact of NFTs?

The environmental impact of NFTs has been a topic of debate. Some NFTs, particularly those minted on the Ethereum blockchain, have been criticized for their energy consumption due to the proof-of-work consensus mechanism. However, there are ongoing efforts to address these concerns, with alternative blockchain solutions and energy-efficient mechanisms being explored.

How can I get started with NFTs?

To start engaging with NFTs, you can create a digital wallet, such as a MetaMask wallet, to store your cryptocurrencies. Next, you can explore various NFT marketplaces (such as OpenSea, Blur, Rarible, Superrare, Makersplace, and Foundation) to browse and purchase NFTs. Keep in mind that due diligence is essential when buying NFTs, and it's crucial to research the artists and verify the authenticity of the artworks.

Is it safe to invest in NFTs?

As with any investment, there are risks associated with investing in NFTs. The NFT market can be volatile, and the prices of digital assets can fluctuate significantly. It's essential to conduct thorough research, seek expert advice, and only invest what you can afford to lose.

How can NFTs be used for charitable purposes?

NFTs have opened up new opportunities for charitable initiatives. Artists and collectors can mint and sell NFTs, with proceeds supporting various causes. Charity auctions and fundraisers are increasingly being conducted using NFTs to raise funds for charitable organizations and projects.

Can NFTs be resold or traded?

Yes, NFTs can be resold or traded on various NFT marketplaces. Owners of NFTs have the flexibility to sell their assets at their desired price, and blockchain ensures a transparent record of ownership transfers.

What is art?

Art is a complex and multifaceted concept that defies a singular definition due to its subjective and ever-evolving nature. At its core, art is a form of creative expression that communicates thoughts, emotions, and ideas through various mediums–visual, auditory, performance-based, and so on.

Art encompasses a wide range of artistic disciplines, including painting, sculpture, drawing, photography, music, dance, literature, film, and theater. Art reflects the human experience, often serving as a mirror to society, culture, history, and personal perspectives.

While the interpretation of art can vary significantly from person to person, it often evokes emotional responses, challenges existing norms, provokes critical thinking and fosters dialogue. Art has the power to inspire, inform, entertain, and evoke a sense of beauty or awe.

Throughout history, art has taken on different forms and styles, influenced by cultural, social, and technological advancements. It can transcend language barriers and connect people across time and space.

Art is not limited to traditional notions of beauty or technical skill. It can also encompass unconventional and experimental forms that challenge traditional boundaries and push the boundaries of what is considered art. The art world is dynamic and ever-evolving, continually embracing new mediums and concepts as artists explore and redefine the boundaries of creativity.

Ultimately, the definition of art is deeply personal and subjective, shaped by individual experiences, perspectives, and cultural backgrounds. It is a testament to the limitless possibilities of human imagination and the power of creativity to shape our understanding of the world.

What is considered tech?

Technology, often referred to as "tech," encompasses a broad range of tools, techniques, systems, and methods used to solve problems, accomplish tasks, and facilitate human activities. It involves the application of scientific knowledge, engineering principles, and practical skills to create, design, develop, and utilize devices, systems, and processes.

Tech can refer to both physical hardware and software components. It includes a vast array of fields and disciplines, such as information technology, computer science, telecommunications, electronics, robotics, AI, biotechnology, and nanotechnology. These fields intersect and overlap, contributing to advancements and innovations in various industries and aspects of daily life.

In today's digital age, tech often refers to digital systems, computer-based applications, software development, internet-related technologies, and emerging technologies like blockchain, virtual reality, augmented reality, and the Internet of Things. Tech plays a crucial role in shaping industries such as communication, transportation, healthcare, entertainment, finance and education.

Tech can be transformative, offering new possibilities, improving efficiency, and driving progress in society. It can enable automation, enhance communication and connectivity, facilitate access to information, empower individuals and communities, and create new opportunities for innovation and growth.

It is important to note that the definition of technology is constantly evolving as new advancements emerge, and existing technologies evolve. What is considered tech today may be different from what was considered tech in the past, and it will continue to evolve as new discoveries and inventions are made.

What is blockchain?

Blockchain is a decentralized digital ledger technology that enables the secure and transparent recording, storing, and verification of transactions or data across multiple computers or nodes. It is often referred to as a distributed ledger technology.

At its core, a blockchain is a chain of blocks, where each block contains a list of transactions or data. These blocks are linked together in chronological order, forming an immutable and transparent record of all the transactions or data that have occurred on the network.

One of the key features of blockchain is decentralization. Unlike traditional centralized systems where a central authority controls and verifies transactions, blockchain operates on a peer-to-peer network, where multiple participants or nodes collectively maintain and validate the integrity of the blockchain.

The decentralized nature of blockchain ensures that no single entity has control over the network, making it more resistant to censorship, manipulation, and single points of failure. It also enhances security, as recorded transactions are secured through advanced cryptographic algorithms.

Another important characteristic of blockchain is transparency. Once a transaction or data is recorded on a blockchain, it becomes visible to all participants on the network. This transparency helps establish trust among participants and provides a verifiable and auditable history of transactions.

Blockchain technology has gained significant attention and adoption beyond its initial application in cryptocurrencies like bitcoin. The technology has found utility in various industries and sectors, including finance, supply chain management, healthcare, voting systems, real estate, and intellectual property. Blockchain's potential lies in its ability to provide secure, transparent, and decentralized solutions that can streamline processes, reduce intermediaries, increase efficiency, and foster trust in digital interactions.

There are different types of blockchains, including public (open to anyone), private (restricted to specific participants), and consortium or hybrid blockchains (a combination of public and private). Each type has its own use cases and considerations, depending on the requirements of the application.

What problems can blockchain solve?

Blockchain technology has the potential to solve various problems across different industries. Some key problems that blockchain can address are listed below.

Trust and Transparency
Blockchain can provide a decentralized and immutable ledger, ensuring transparency and accountability in transactions. This eliminates the need for intermediaries or trusted third parties, reducing the risk of fraud, manipulation, or corruption.

Security and Data Integrity
Blockchain utilizes cryptographic techniques to secure transactions and data. It offers a tamper-resistant and auditable record, protecting against unauthorized access, data tampering, and cyberattacks.

Streamlining Processes and Efficiency

Blockchain can automate and streamline complex processes by removing manual, time-consuming, and error-prone intermediaries. It enables faster, more efficient, and cost-effective transactions, reducing delays and paperwork.

Supply Chain Traceability

Blockchain can enhance supply chain transparency by tracking and recording the movement of goods, ensuring authenticity, verifying origins, and reducing counterfeiting. It enables stakeholders to have a real-time view of the supply chain, improving efficiency and trust.

Data Privacy and Ownership

Blockchain allows individuals to have control over their personal data. It enables secure storage and sharing of and consent-based access to data, giving individuals ownership and control over their digital identities.

Financial Inclusion

Blockchain can provide access to financial services for the unbanked and underbanked populations. It enables peer-to-peer transactions, reduces transaction costs, and facilitates cross-border payments, empowering individuals in underserved regions.

Smart Contracts and Automation

Blockchain supports the execution of self-executing smart contracts, which are programmable agreements that automatically execute when predefined conditions are met. Smart contracts can automate processes, reduce the need for intermediaries, and ensure transparent and reliable agreements.

Decentralization and Resilience

Blockchain's decentralized nature ensures that no single entity has control over the network. This resilience makes it more resistant to censorship, single points of failure, and data loss, improving system robustness and reliability.

What is Ethereum?

Ethereum is an open-source blockchain platform that enables the creation and execution of decentralized applications (dApps) and smart contracts. It was proposed by Vitalik Buterin in late 2013 and developed in 2014 with the goal of expanding the capabilities of blockchain beyond simple peer-to-peer transactions.

Unlike Bitcoin, which primarily focuses on being a digital currency, Ethereum provides a more flexible and programmable environment for developers to build and deploy dApps. It introduced the concept of smart contracts, which are self-executing agreements with the terms of the contract directly written into code. These smart contracts automatically execute when specific conditions are met, removing the need for intermediaries or third parties.

Ethereum's native cryptocurrency is called ether (ETH), which serves as the fuel for running dApps on the Ethereum platform. Ether is used to incentivize participants to validate transactions and execute smart contracts.

One of the key features of Ethereum is its Turing-complete virtual machine–called the Ethereum Virtual Machine which allows developers to write and deploy smart contracts in various programming languages. It provides a secure and sandboxed environment for executing code, ensuring that smart contracts run exactly as intended without the risk of external interference.

Ethereum has played a significant role in the growth of the decentralized finance (DeFi) ecosystem, enabling the development of financial applications such as decentralized exchanges, lending platforms, and stablecoins. It has also facilitated the emergence of NFTs, which are unique digital assets that can represent ownership of artwork, collectibles, and more.

Ethereum has undergone several upgrades to enhance its scalability, security, and functionality. The most notable upgrade is Ethereum 2.0, also known as Ethereum's transition to a proof-of-stake consensus mechanism. This upgrade aims to improve scalability and energy efficiency, making the Ethereum network more sustainable and capable of handling a larger number of transactions.

Overall, Ethereum has become a prominent platform for blockchain-based applications, smart contracts, and digital assets, fostering innovation and enabling new possibilities in decentralized computing.

What is NFT, and who invented it?

NFT stands for Non-Fungible Token. It is a type of digital asset that represents ownership or proof of authenticity of a unique item or piece of content, such as an artwork, a collectible, music, a video, or virtual real estate. Unlike cryptocurrencies such as bitcoin and Ethereum, which are fungible and can be exchanged on a one-to-one basis, each NFT is distinct and cannot be exchanged on a like-for-like basis.

NFTs are built on blockchain technology, typically using platforms such as Ethereum, and are stored on a public ledger, providing a transparent and verifiable record of ownership. This ensures the scarcity, provenance, and authenticity of the digital asset, making it valuable to collectors and enthusiasts.

The concept of NFTs was first proposed and implemented on the Ethereum blockchain. While there is no single person credited with inventing NFTs, the development of the ERC-721 standard on Ethereum played a pivotal role in popularizing the idea and creating a standardized framework for NFTs.

ERC-721, introduced by Dieter Shirley and William Entriken, was first proposed in 2017 as a token standard that allows for the creation and ownership of unique digital assets on the Ethereum blockchain. The standard defines the basic functionality and characteristics of NFTs, enabling developers to create and interact with them in a standardized way.

One of the early implementations of ERC-721 was the CryptoKitties project, developed by Axiom Zen in late 2017. CryptoKitties introduced the concept of collectible digital cats, each representing a unique NFT. The game gained significant attention and became one of the first mainstream applications of NFTs, highlighting the potential for digital ownership and collectibles on blockchain.

Since then, NFTs have grown in popularity and have been adopted by various artists, creators, and developers across different industries. The market for NFTs has expanded rapidly, with new platforms, marketplaces, and applications emerging to support the buying, selling, and trading of unique digital assets.

It is important to note that while the concept of unique digital ownership existed before NFTs, the implementation of blockchain technology and the standardization through ERC-721 and subsequent improvements have been instrumental in shaping the NFT landscape we see today.

What can be considered a digital asset?

A digital asset is any item or piece of content that exists in digital form and holds value or represents ownership or rights. It refers to a wide range of intangible assets that can be stored, transferred, and accessed electronically. Here are some examples of digital assets:

Digital Art
Digital artworks, illustrations, animations, and other forms of digital creative expressions can be considered digital assets. With the rise of NFTs, digital art has gained recognition and value in the digital space.

Music and Audio Files
Digital music tracks, albums, podcasts, audiobooks, and other audio content stored in digital formats like MP3 and WAV or on streaming services are digital assets. Each individual song or audio file can be considered a unique digital asset.

Videos and Films
Digital videos, movies, TV shows, documentaries, and other video content are digital assets. These can be stored as files in various formats, streamed online, or distributed through digital platforms.

E-books and Digital Publications
Books, magazines, newspapers, and other written content in digital formats, such as PDF and EPUB, are digital assets. They can be downloaded, accessed, and read on electronic devices.

Software and Applications
Computer programs, mobile applications, and software licenses are digital assets. They are intangible and can be downloaded, installed, and used on electronic devices.

Domain Names

Website addresses or domain names are digital assets that represent the online identities of individuals, businesses, or organizations. They can be bought, sold, and transferred.

Cryptocurrencies

Cryptocurrencies like bitcoin and Ethereum are digital assets that exist on blockchain networks. They hold value and can be used as a medium of exchange or investment.

Virtual Real Estate

Virtual lands, properties, and spaces in online virtual worlds or games can be considered digital assets. These assets can be bought, sold, or rented within the virtual environment.

Collectibles and Trading Cards

Digital collectibles, trading cards, and virtual items on gaming or blockchain-based platforms are digital assets. They can have unique attributes, scarcity, and value within their respective ecosystems.

Digital Tickets

Tickets to events, concerts, movies, or sports games that are stored and accessed digitally on mobile devices or online platforms are digital assets. They represent proof of entry or ownership for a specific event.

Digital Identity

Digital identity documents like passports, driver's licenses, and digital IDs stored and verified electronically are digital assets that represent personal identity and credentials.

Virtual Avatars and Characters

Digital representations of individuals in virtual worlds, video games, or augmented reality experiences can be considered digital assets. They often hold customization options, unique attributes, and personalization.

Digital Reputation and Social Capital
Online ratings, reviews, endorsements, and social media followers can be considered digital assets that contribute to an individual's or brand's online reputation and influence.

Data and Datasets
Digital datasets, research findings, scientific papers, and big data analytics can be considered digital assets. They hold valuable information and insights that can be utilized for various purposes.

Digital Securities
Digitally represented securities, such as stocks, bonds, or investment contracts, are digital assets that can be bought, sold, and traded in digital marketplaces.

What is Web3?

Web3 refers to the vision and concept of the next generation of the internet, which is focused on decentralization, user ownership, and increased privacy. Web3 is often associated with blockchain technology and cryptocurrencies. While the current version of the internet, Web 2, is characterized by centralized platforms, data silos, and limited user control, Web3 aims to create a more open, transparent, and user-centric digital ecosystem.

Web3 introduces the concept of dApps that run on blockchain networks, allowing users to interact with services and platforms without relying on intermediaries or central authorities. These dApps leverage smart contracts. This enables the automation of transactions and eliminates the need for traditional intermediaries.

The core principles of Web3 include the following:

Decentralization
Web3 aims to distribute power and control among network participants, reducing reliance on centralized authorities. Blockchain technology plays a vital role in achieving this decentralization by providing a transparent and immutable ledger for transactions and data storage.

User Ownership and Control
Web3 emphasizes user ownership and control over their data, digital assets, and online identities. Through the use of cryptographic keys and wallets, individuals can have full control over their digital assets, participate in decentralized governance, and selectively share their personal information.

Interoperability
Web3 envisions a future where different blockchain networks and dApps can seamlessly interact and exchange information. This interoperability allows for the creation of a unified and interconnected decentralized ecosystem.

Privacy and Security
Web3 emphasizes enhanced privacy and security through cryptographic techniques. Users have more control over their personal data and can choose to share it in a pseudonymous or anonymous manner. This shift reduces the risk of data breaches and unauthorized access.

Tokenization
Web3 leverages tokens, often in the form of cryptocurrencies or utility tokens, to represent and facilitate the exchange of value within the ecosystem. These tokens enable new economic models, incentivize user participation, and provide mechanisms for

decentralized governance.

Web3 has the potential to transform various industries beyond finance, such as art, gaming, supply chain management, and social media. It empowers individuals, promotes trust, and fosters innovation by providing a more inclusive and user-centric digital environment.

Why do brands want to adopt Web3?

Brands are increasingly interested in entering the Web3 space for several reasons:

Access to a New Audience
Web3 and blockchain technologies have attracted a growing community of early adopters and tech-savvy individuals. By establishing a presence in the Web3 space, brands can reach and engage with this new audience, expanding their customer base and tapping into a demographic that values decentralization, transparency, and user control.

Innovation and Differentiation
Web3 offers brands an opportunity to leverage cutting-edge technologies and explore innovative business models. By embracing dApps, blockchain-based solutions, and tokenization, brands can differentiate themselves in the market, showcase their forward-thinking approach, and stand out from competitors.

Enhanced Trust and Transparency
Web3 technology, with its focus on decentralization and immutable records, can help brands enhance trust and transparency in their operations. By leveraging blockchain for supply chain management, for example, brands can provide verifiable proof of authenticity, traceability, and ethical sourcing. This can resonate with consumers who prioritize transparency and social

responsibility.

Engagement and Community Building

Web3 platforms often foster strong communities and active participation. Brands can leverage these platforms to engage directly with their customers, encourage user-generated content, and build deeper connections. This increased engagement can lead to brand loyalty, advocacy, and valuable feedback for product development and improvement.

New Revenue Streams

Web3 introduces new economic models and opportunities for brands to generate revenue. By tokenizing their products or services, brands can create digital assets that have value within the Web3 ecosystem. These assets can be bought, sold, and traded, potentially creating new revenue streams and monetization avenues.

Partnerships and Collaborations

The Web3 space is a hub for collaboration and partnerships. Brands can collaborate with blockchain projects, dApps, and other Web3 initiatives to co-create innovative solutions or tap into existing networks and user bases. These collaborations can lead to shared expertise, increased brand exposure, and access to new markets.

Increased Data Security

Web3 technologies, such as blockchain, offer enhanced data security compared to traditional centralized systems. By leveraging decentralized networks and cryptographic techniques, brands can protect sensitive user data from breaches, hacking, and unauthorized access. This heightened data security can foster trust among consumers, especially in an era of increasing concerns about data privacy.

Tokenized Loyalty Programs

Brands can leverage Web3 to create tokenized loyalty programs, where customers earn digital tokens or rewards that hold value within the ecosystem. These tokens can be used for various purposes, such as exclusive access to products or services, discounts, or even governance rights within the brand's ecosystem. Tokenized loyalty programs can incentivize customer engagement, strengthen brand loyalty, and create a sense of exclusivity.

Innovative Marketing and Advertising

Web3 introduces new possibilities for marketing and advertising campaigns. Organizations can leverage NFTs to create unique digital assets tied to their brand, which can be used for promotional purposes or as collectibles. Additionally, Web3 platforms often incorporate decentralized advertising models that prioritize user consent, fair compensation for attention, and more targeted ad delivery.

Immutable Brand Identity and Intellectual Property

Web3 technologies can help protect and authenticate brand identity and intellectual property. By utilizing blockchain-based systems, brands can establish permanent records of their trademarks, copyrights, and other assets, ensuring provable ownership and reducing the risk of counterfeiting or infringement. This enables brands to reinforce their authenticity and safeguard their intellectual property rights.

DeFi Participation

Brands can explore opportunities in the burgeoning DeFi field within the Web3 space. By integrating DeFi protocols, brands can offer innovative financial services, such as decentralized lending, insurance, or investment opportunities. This allows them to tap into the growing interest in DeFi and attract customers who seek decentralized and permissionless financial solutions.

How likely is it for NFTs and Web3 to cool off and eventually die?

Here are a few reasons it is unlikely for NFTs and Web3 to completely cool off and die:

Growing Adoption and Mainstream Interest

NFTs and Web3 have gained significant traction and attention from mainstream media, artists, brands, and investors. Major companies, celebrities, and established institutions have embraced NFTs and blockchain technology, indicating a growing acceptance and interest. This level of adoption suggests the continued presence and evolution of the technology.

Evolving Infrastructure and Applications

The infrastructure and ecosystem supporting NFTs and Web3 are constantly evolving and improving. Developers, entrepreneurs, and innovators are actively building new platforms, applications, and use cases within the Web3 space. As the technology matures, we can expect more sophisticated solutions, improved user experiences, and wider adoption across industries.

Diverse Use Cases beyond Art

While NFTs initially gained prominence in the art world, they have already expanded into various other sectors, including gaming, virtual real estate, collectibles and music. The versatility of NFTs and their potential for digital ownership and provenance make them applicable to a wide range of assets and industries. This diversification of use cases strengthens the overall resilience of NFTs and Web3.

Community and Cultural Shift

NFTs and Web3 have created vibrant communities of artists, collectors, developers, and enthusiasts. These communities actively contribute to the growth, development, and sustainability of the technology. The shared values of decentralization, ownership, and community-driven governance provide a strong foundation for continued innovation and engagement.

Blockchain's Inherent Advantages

The underlying technology of blockchain provides inherent advantages such as transparency, immutability, and security. These features address key pain points in various industries, including provenance, authenticity, and trust. As long as the benefits of blockchain technology remain relevant, it is likely to continue to be embraced and integrated into various applications, including NFTs.

A comparison of the environmental impacts of traditional and digital art

Resource Consumption

Traditional art often requires physical supplies such as canvases, paints, brushes, and sculptures, made from various materials. The production and disposal of these materials can have environmental consequences, including resource extraction, energy consumption during manufacturing, and waste generation. In contrast, digital art and NFTs primarily rely on digital tools and platforms, which have a lower physical resource footprint.

Transportation and Storage

Traditional art often requires transportation for exhibitions, auctions, and storage in galleries or private collections. This involves packaging, shipping, and sometimes international travel, which contribute to carbon emissions and energy consumption. Digital art and NFTs, on the other hand, can be instantly accessible and shared globally without the need for physical transportation or storage.

Replication and Conservation

Traditional art involves creating physical copies, reproductions, and limited editions. These processes require additional resources and may contribute to the creation of more physical objects. In contrast, digital art and NFTs can be easily replicated and shared digitally, thus reducing the need for physical copies and conserving resources.

Longevity and Preservation

Traditional art often requires preservation efforts to maintain its quality and integrity over time. This includes climate-controlled storage, restoration, and conservation practices, which can have associated environmental impacts. Digital art and NFTs, when stored and backed up properly, can potentially have longer lifespans and require fewer physical preservation efforts.

Carbon Footprint

The carbon footprint of digital art and NFTs is often a point of contention. While the process of minting NFTs on certain blockchains, such as Ethereum, can consume a significant amount of energy, it is important to consider the overall carbon footprint of the entire traditional art ecosystem, including the production, transportation, and storage aspects mentioned earlier.

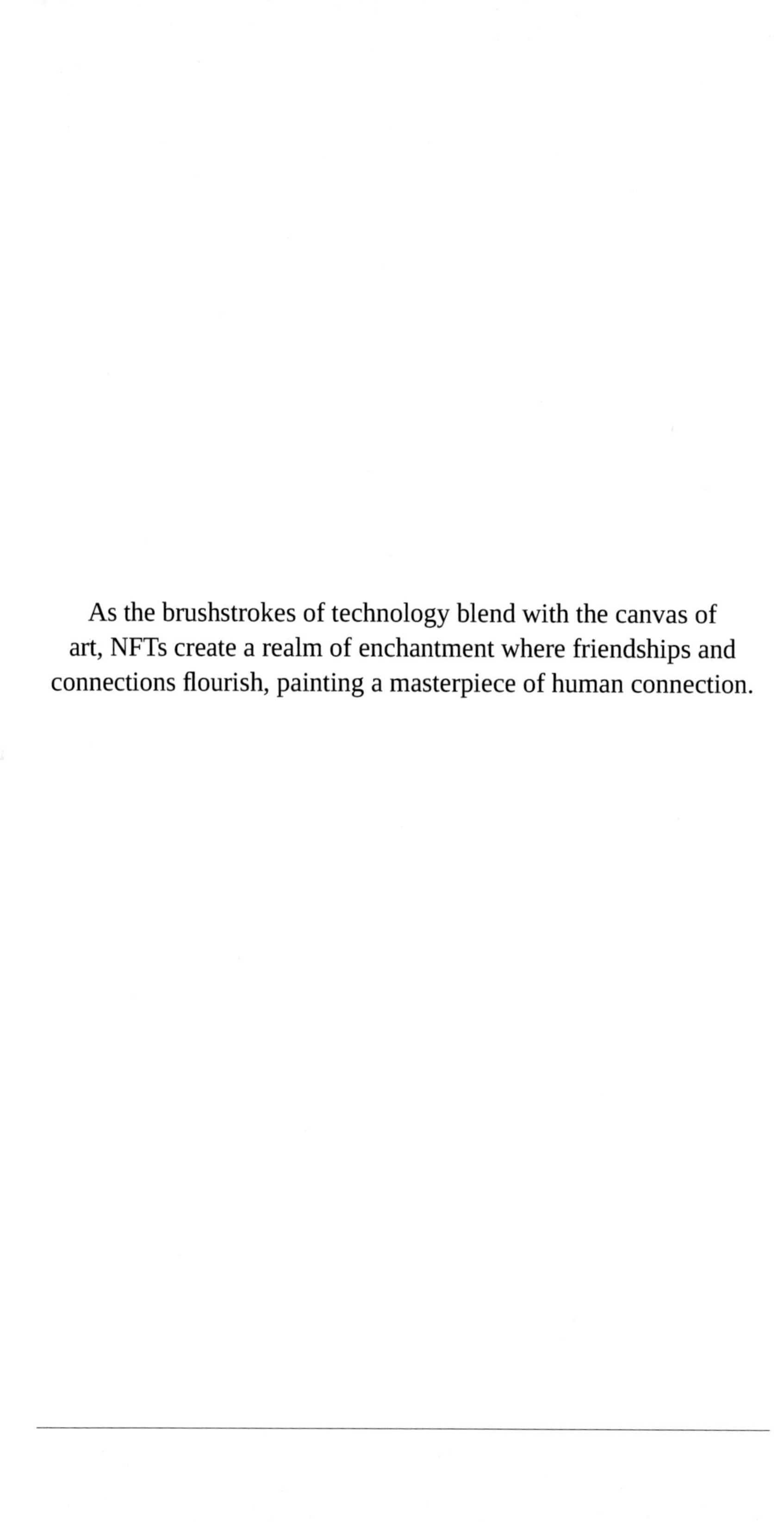

As the brushstrokes of technology blend with the canvas of art, NFTs create a realm of enchantment where friendships and connections flourish, painting a masterpiece of human connection.

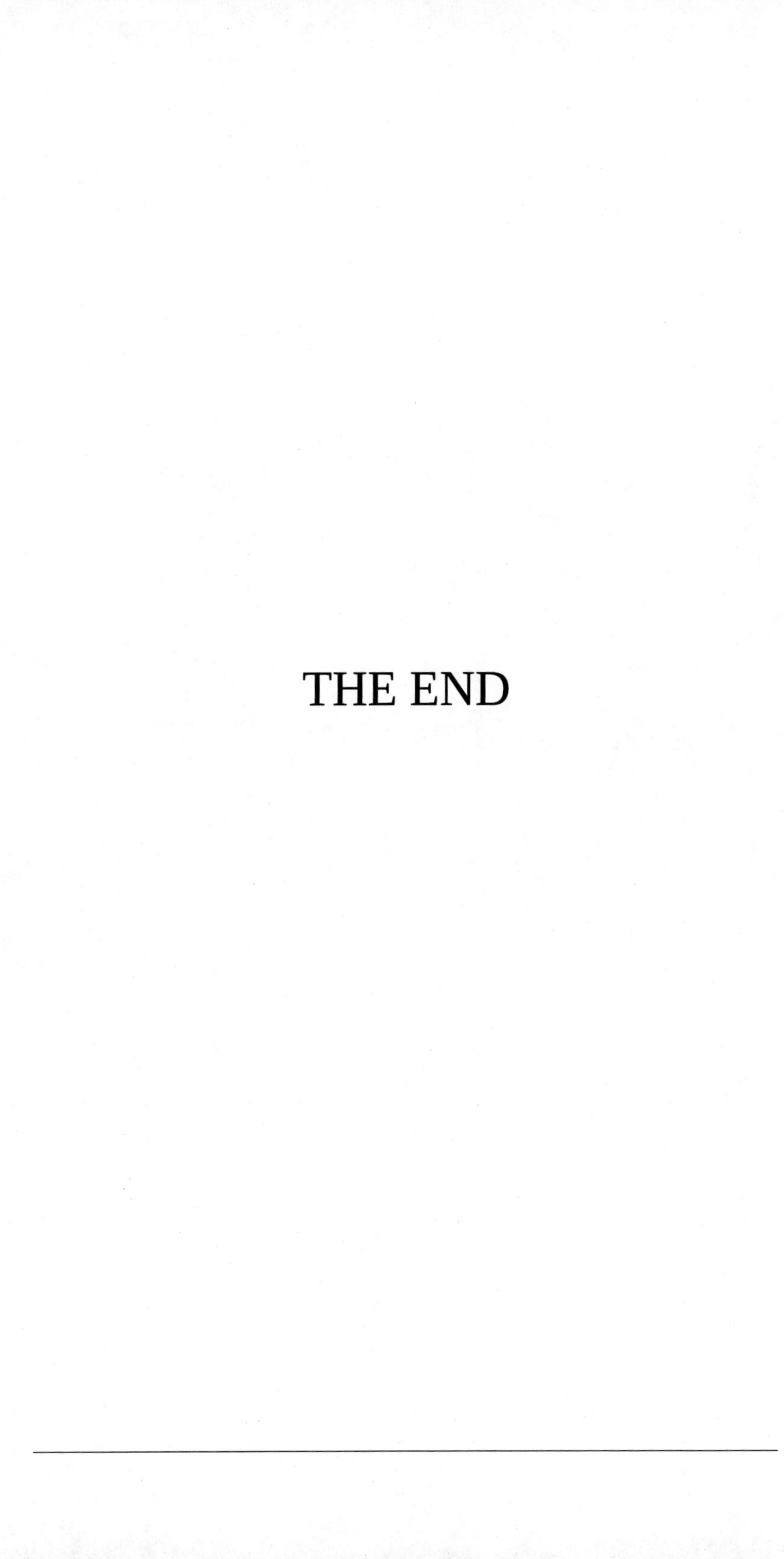

THE END

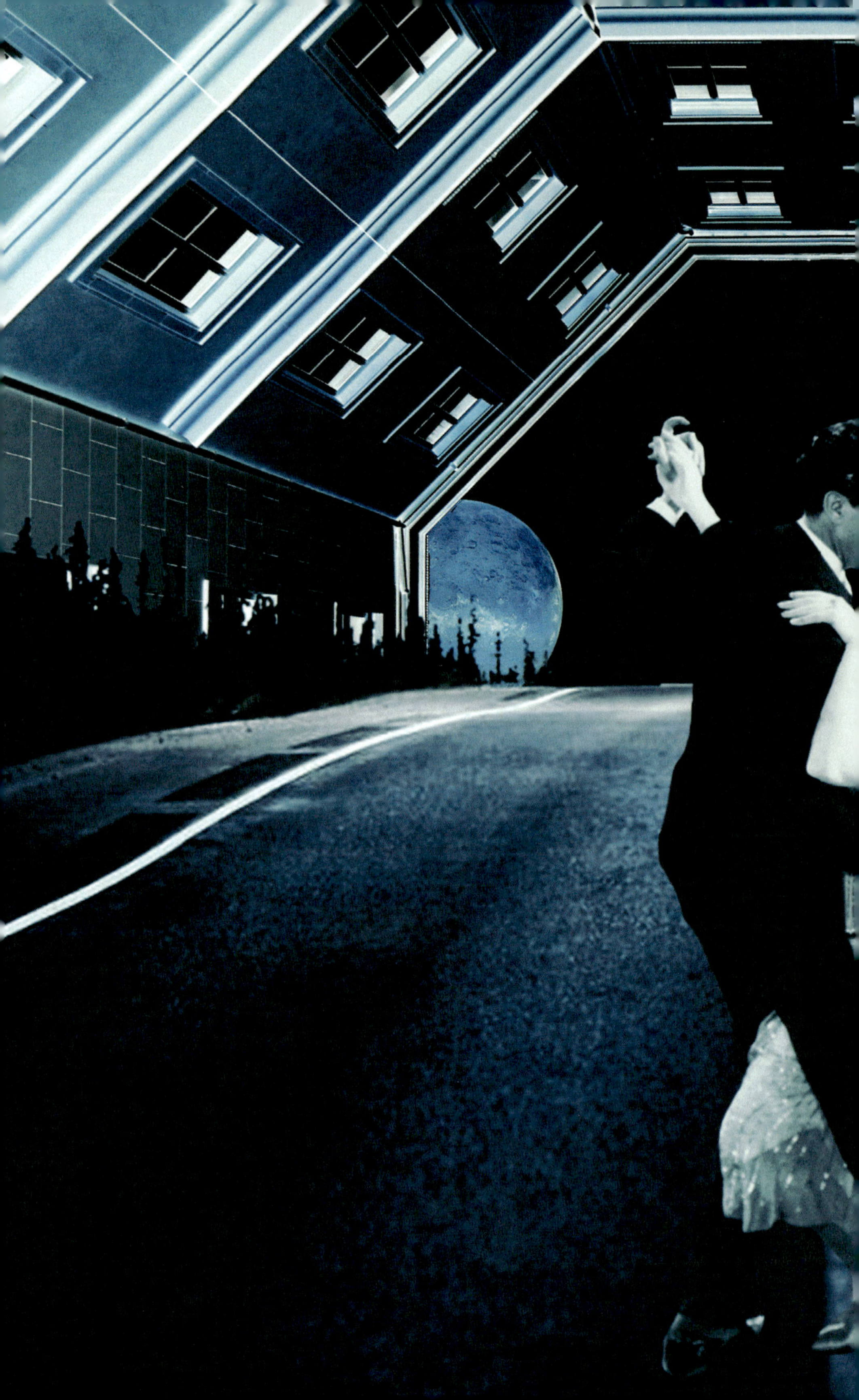

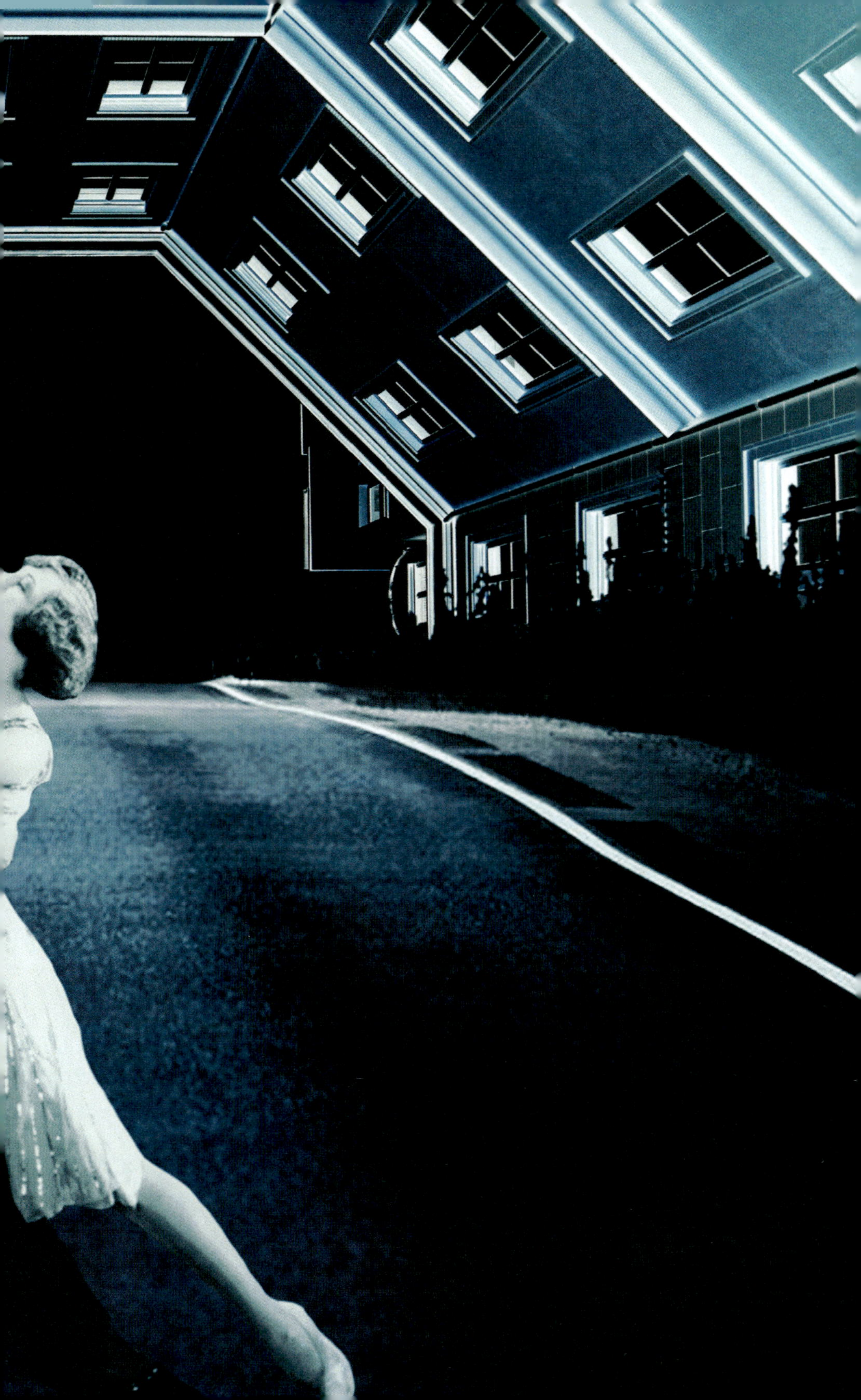

Bio

Amir “Mondoir” Soleymani, a visionary entrepreneur and art enthusiast, is a trailblazer in the world of non-fungible tokens (NFTs) and blockchain technology. With a passion for democratizing the art world, Amir’s journey into the NFT space began as a fascination with the intersection of art and technology, leading to a profound exploration of the transformative power of NFTs.

As an early adopter, Amir established himself as a prominent figure in the NFT community, forging invaluable connections with artists, collectors, and thought leaders.

Amir’s art collection reflects a narrative of diverse voices and creative visions, representing the intersection of artistry and innovation. As an entrepreneur, Amir has played a significant role in shaping the NFT landscape and building platforms to foster artist discovery and collaboration.

In this book, *The Art of Connectivity: Unveiling the Magic of NFTs*, Amir offers readers profound insights into the world of NFTs, inspiring art enthusiasts to embrace this digital revolution and unlock the boundless potential of the art world in the age of Web3.

Follow Amir on Twitter (X) at @mondoir for the latest updates. Learn more about Amir and the team at www.mondoir.com.

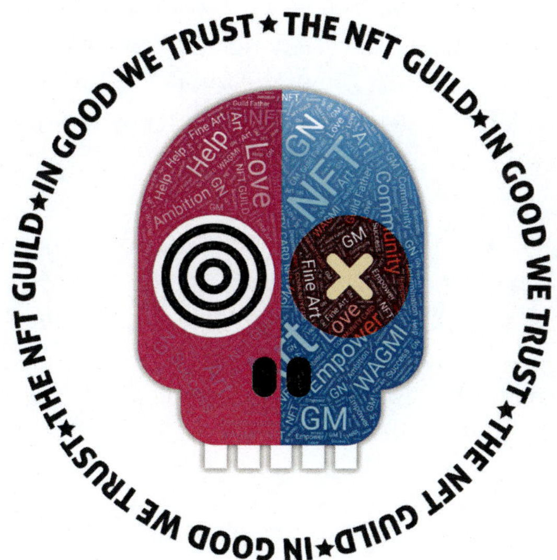

Proof of Reading Collectible

Dear Reader,

Upon completing the book, I would like to extend my gratitude by offering you a complimentary digital collectible as a token of appreciation. The process is hassle-free, and you do not require a digital wallet to participate. However, if you do have one, you can transfer the collectible to your wallet after it's minted.

To begin, simply scan the QR code below, which will direct you to the claim page. After providing your email address, your Proof of Reading collectible will be minted on the Polygon blockchain and sent directly to your email. Please double-check your email address, as there is no way to recover the minted NFT if an incorrect email address is provided. I want to ensure that you receive your collectible without any issues.

Please note that this Proof of Reading collectible holds no financial value and should be regarded solely as a heartfelt gesture of appreciation for your time and commitment to reading the book.

Thank you again for being a valued reader, and I hope you enjoy your new digital collectible.

Made in the USA
Monee, IL
14 August 2023

8b560e84-0b0a-4aff-b61b-f4e83df1650cR01